EPIPHANY OF A MIDDLE~AGED PILGRIM

essays in lieu of a memoir

PETER WORTSMAN

Epiphany of a Middle-Aged Pilgrim by Peter Wortsman

ISBN: 978-1-949790-47-4

eISBN: 978-1-949790-48-1

Cover Design: Harold Wortsman

Author photo: © 2016 Ricky Owens
Layout and book design by Mark Givens

First Pelekinesis Printing 2021

For information:
Pelekinesis, 112 Harvard Ave #65, Claremont, CA 91711 USA

Library of Congress Cataloging-in-Publication Data

Names: Wortsman, Peter, author.
Title: Epiphany of a middle-aged pilgrim : essays in lieu of a memoir / Peter Wortsman.
Description: Claremont : Pelekinesis, 2021. | Summary: "In the short personal essays that comprise Epiphany of a Middle-Aged Pilgrim, Essays in lieu of a Memoir, author Peter Wortsman, best known for his original prose fiction and stage plays, and his translations from the German, follows in the footsteps of French essayist Michel de Montaigne, taking stock of life in middle age. His perspectives, including childhood fear, chronic insomnia, ironing a shirt, getting a haircut, having a skin cancer removed, travel at home and abroad, a consciousness of getting older, et al, and concluding with a reflection of life in lockdown during the Covid-19 pandemic, make for a rich mosaic of memories meant to spur readers to seek out their own epiphanies"-- Provided by publisher.
Identifiers: LCCN 2021026556 (print) | LCCN 2021026557 (ebook) | ISBN 9781949790474 (paperback) | ISBN 9781949790481 (epub)
Subjects: LCSH: Wortsman, Peter. | Authors, American--20th century--Biography.
Classification: LCC PS3573.O77 E65 2021 (print) | LCC PS3573.O77 (ebook) | DDC 813/.54--dc23
LC record available at https://lccn.loc.gov/2021026556
LC ebook record available at https://lccn.loc.gov/2021026557

www.pelekinesis.com

Epiphany of a Middle-Aged Pilgrim

essays in lieu of a memoir

PETER WORTSMAN

To my wife, Claudie, and my brother, Harold,
who can read me like a book

Contents

III Epiphanies of the Palate

IV Notes of a Native Stranger

V Far and Wide

"We are fashioned out of oddments put together."
—Michel Eyquem de Montaigne

"Most of life's epiphanies arise from its accidents ..."
—Murray Kempton

Embracing Doubt, or How I Learned to Love the Semi-Colon
(A Foreword)

The personal essay, as opposed to the story, is supposed to strictly adhere to the stuff of truth. But as soon as the tongue wags, it inevitably embellishes, transforms and frames experience, uplifting life into legend.

In lieu of a proper memoir, I have assembled this book of brief statements about myself in an effort, not to harness memories, but to cast them off as burdensome ballast, and thereby lighten the load of that wobbly hot air balloon bobbing between my shoulders, to make room for however much present the future still holds in store.

Having arrived at a stage of life euphemistically referred to as late middle age, the balance of consciousness inevitably shifts from the comforting illusion of the cup half empty to the disquieting soupçon of the cup half full.

Forgetting is a fact of life. All too often you can't find the right word or forget the name of someone you've known for years. The amygdala, the hippocampus, the cerebellum, and the prefrontal cortex, those storehouses of memory, are rickety receptacles at best. Much falls through the cracks.

The only difference between then and now is an accumulation of doubt. But doubt need not necessarily be debilitating.

I dedicate these musings to the defining punctuation mark of middle age: the semicolon, a veritable hallmark of uncertainty.

Consider the magnanimity of that mongrel hybrid of

comma and period; a philosophical point of punctuation which the wise old King Solomon might well have taken as his coat of arms had it been invented in his day, as it condones, indeed consecrates, hesitation and doubt, permitting a notion once entertained to be nursed, and leaving you comfortable in the knowledge that, though not done with it yet, each conceptual strand spun out of mind can be intertwined with yet another, the warp and woof of which teased out; or to radically shift metaphor, the semicolon is a syntactical railroad switch judiciously deployed to let a train of thought switch tracks, slow down for an uphill trek, and accelerate for the final run into the terminus where it brakes with a hiss and a period.

I

Time Out

First Memory

We are driving over a drawbridge across a body of water — a neck of the Long Island Sound, most likely, but I can't say for certain — in our battered old maroon red-colored car, with my father at the wheel, a lit cigarette jutting from his lips, smoke rising in curlicues above his head, my mother beside me in the back seat, to my left, my older brother to my right. We've been waiting a long while to let a boat pass below, and now we're finally moving. I must be less than three years old, because my little sister isn't in the picture yet. A metallic vibration runs up between my legs, engendering a strange tingle, as the tires roll over the teeth of the bridge's supine uplift structure.

The rudimentary principles of a drawbridge must have been explained to me, as I remember being puzzled to the point of panic, attempting to fathom how a structure ordinarily conceived to transport people and cars safely over water could split neatly down the middle, lift to let a boat pass under, and then fall safely back into place. The panic strains my primitive capacity for logical thought, prompting the release of the floodwaters below.

—"Pipi, Mama!"

—"Wait!"

She can tell from my desperate expression, lips pressed tightly together, eyes shut tight, that my recently acquired mastery of bladder control is tenuous at best, and that release is imminent. My mother is prepared, with lightning speed she reaches down with her left hand and grabs hold of an empty milk bottle reserved for that express purpose that had been rolling around at her feet, while with her right she skillfully unzips my fly and pulls out the little hose called a *Schwoferl* in our immigrant family lingo, for which I do not as yet possess an English word — a body part the sight of which sends adults into peals of laughter — and guides its tip into the mouth of the empty milk bottle just in the nick of time.

Yellow panic comes spurting out.

The Bridge crossing doesn't take long — but for me it's a tiny eternity, the relief is profound, the angst stilled, the tingle, a not altogether disagreeable sensation, mingling with the memory of it.

Fear Eats Soul[1]

As a child I coddle fear. Perhaps it is an internalized response to my parents' experience, as escapees from Nazi-occupied Austria, an unconscious attempt to live up to what they'd lived through. For years my nightmares invariably involve being chased by black-booted goons, shooting awake in a cold sweat, relieved, but also secretly disappointed, to find myself safe under the covers. Perhaps it is a function of the moment, the late 1950s and early 60s, a time of optimism and prosperity, tempered somewhat by Cold War dread that reaches its crescendo in the Cuban Missile Crisis, when we crouch under our desks in school with our hands folded over our heads, waiting for the world to blow up. Perhaps it is just the high-strung temperament of a little boy with a dark imagination.

Fear is my constant companion. Fear of a calamity befalling me as soon as I leave the safety of my bedroom. The threat of some impending disaster makes me tremble, but also adds a certain drama and purpose to an otherwise uneventful life.

I develop a tried-and-true ritual for forestalling, if not eluding, certain disaster. As soon as I am washed and dressed and out the door on the way to school every weekday morning, I promptly vomit all over myself, making sure to so thoroughly soil my clothes that my mother has to take me back home to

---

[1] The title of this essay is borrowed from that of German filmmaker Rainer Werner Fassbinder's 1974 film *Angst Essen Seele auf,* roughly rendered in English as "Fear Eats the Soul," but more accurately translated as the more awkward agrammatical "Fear Eats Soul."

get changed.

My actual fears seem paltry in retrospect: the fear of wetting my pants, or worse, letting go with number two. The toilet stalls in the boys' room at school lack doors, and therefore, rather than be caught with my pants down, I hold it in all day. But a child's terror can attain monumental proportions.

Fear finds a home at the apartment of my father's stepmother, Jenny, on Manhattan's Upper West Side. My father was already an adult by the time his father remarried, though Jenny had apparently been Grandfather's mistress for years. And though my father's feelings for her were hardly filial, blaming her, I'm quite sure, for his mother's distress and early demise, Jenny had never had children of her own, and so, after his father's passing, to make amends for his lack of affection, my father would occasionally leave us children in her care while he and my mother went shopping, caught a movie, or just took a stroll down Broadway.

A woman with arms as thick as her thighs, a halo of unruly white hair, and a volcanic laugh more like a purging than a burst of merriment, she is a character of fairy tale aura and proportions. She always serves us baked apples, which, being a finicky eater, I pick at, but refuse to taste, on account of their blanched color and shriveled consistency, a dish in my eyes resembling condensed children's skulls, that might well have emerged from the witch's oven in Hansel and Gretel.

Once we are done eating, or in my case fidgeting around and poking with my fork at the decomposed skin of baked apples, Jenny seeks to distract my brother, sister and myself with accounts of a camp for naughty children whose very name, Unterkralawitz, which she elongates in the telling, trilling her r's, sends us into peals of anxious laughter. The camp is run by the heartless head mistress, Frau Posposchil. And discipline is meted out without redress by the dreaded Dr. Hagatai, who wears a top hat twice his size and wields a big long stick with which, when instructed to do so by the head mistress, he metes out punishment, beating disobedient boys and girls black and blue. When pressed as to whether such a place really exists, or whether she'd made it up, Jenny, a refugee herself, just winks. Though we children don't really believe in its reality, she solemnly warns that if we're bad, we'll end up there. My parents maintain the tongue-in-cheek fiction, by inference extending the threat to all summer camps, to be avoided at all costs.

Once back home, when climbing on a chair and reaching for a paperback on my father's shelf, among the books off-limits to us children, *The Pictorial History of the Third Reich*, I happen upon the picture of a camp with gaunt, hollow-eyed stick figures peering out and others lying still beside them. The last three letters of the name in the caption "itz," rhyme with the last letters of Jenny's grim locale.

I recently searched the internet, and found an obscure reference in a Roster of Royal Laws of the erstwhile Austro-Hungarian Empire to a reform school in a place called Unterkralawitz in the former Kingdom of Bohemia.

Jenny wasn't kidding after all.

Like Father, Like Son

The culture of birthing is different in France. At our first visit to a Parisian obstetrician recommended by friends, my French wife assures him that, of course, she abstains from wine and coffee, as she'd been counseled to do by her American doctor.

"Oh?" observes the puzzled Gallic practitioner with eyebrows arched in circumflex accents of concern. "A glass of good red Bordeaux with supper is very nutritious, and a cup of coffee in the morning can surely do no harm."

And once, when selecting cheeses at the covered market near where we lived at the time, upon seeking assurance, again on her American doctor's advice, that they are pasteurized, my wife elicits a stern tongue lashing from the deadpan proprietress of the dairy stand. "If you want pasteurized cheese," she snaps, "better get it at the supermarket!"

My wife's pregnancy goes well, all things considered, until the due date draws near, and I hold our little daughter by the hand, and haul our suitcases onto a speed train headed south to my wife's hometown, Valence, where she chose to give birth, leaving her to contend, kangaroo-like, with her bulging built-in baggage.

It is a relatively smooth and speedy delivery, a matter of a couple of hours, unlike the twelve hours it had taken for our daughter to emerge five years before in a New York maternity ward. My late, beloved father-in-law and I share the potent Cuban cigars I procured for the occasion. And unlike the slam-bam-thankyou, ma'am-24-hour-time-allotment of the American healthcare system for labor and delivery, healing time included for post-op stitches to a vaginal tear, though there are no complications this time, the French system allots an entire week's stay in the hospital to recoup her strength, and would surely have let her stay longer, had I not pleaded with her to come home, or rather to my late in-laws' house, where we are camped out, and where, fond as I am of them, I have had my fill of being counseled at every turn, reduced to a second childhood.

Our offspring having been born a male, there is still the little problem of the circumcision. Religiously unobservant Jew though I be, I feel a fierce tribal attachment. My wife, an open-minded French intellectual, and self-described "atheist of Catholic culture," understands and accedes to my wish to have our son circumcised, so that, as I put it, "when we pee together, our shlongs will look alike."

By French law, however, a circumcision can only be performed at the public hospital if deemed a medical necessity. There are private clinics that perform the procedure on request, but the public hospital is the more dependable option in France. We call the local Jewish community, but by Jewish law, if the mother is not Jewish, neither is the son. Our newborn would have to convert first, they say. Not a viable option for an apostate Jew like myself with strong tribal ties and an atheist of Catholic culture like my wife! After much fretting and hair pulling, we finally track down and manage to make contact with a liberal Jewish congregation in Lyon, the nearest metropolis. Explaining my quandary—that I feel Jewish by culture, not by religion, and that my wife and I want our son to be circumcised, but without any religious ritual—I am referred to a certain Dr. B., a respected pediatric surgeon and practicing *mohel*,[1] who lives in Paris, whose daughter, by the way, is the first female rabbi to officiate in France. Following a long, drawn-out philosophical dialogue by phone, though he does not share my point of view, he appreciates my position, and kindly agrees to do as we wish, to perform a circumcision without ritual or prayer.

So, in addition to the very reasonable fee for the procedure, we pay his round-trip fare by speed train, and the operation is set to take place in the parlor of my in-laws' house. Upon fathoming just what lies ahead, my father-in-law paces anxiously around the garden, convinced his otherwise level-headed son-in-law has suddenly gone stark raving mad, a cross between Attila the Hun and the heartless Pharaoh in the Bible who orders the slaughter of the innocents, and convinced that his first and only grandson is about to be disfigured.

I had never attended another circumcision, except my own, of which, fortunately, I have no memory. It is customary that the child be held by another family member, while the father stands by. But under the circumstances, there is no one else to hold my son but me. I assume that it is going to be a rapid procedure, with a few drops of blood and all forgotten in a matter of seconds.

But when the blood begins to spill at that most sensitive place in my little son's anatomy, I am gripped by horror and terror. What if the *mohel*'s knife slips! What if he's damaged, mutilated!

And then and there I slip back in time five thousand and some years. I am the Patriarch Abraham summoned by a fierce

---

[1] A ritual practitioner of circumcision, according to Jewish law

deity to do the unthinkable on the summit of Mount Moriah to test my faith, but the angelic messenger hasn't shown up in the nick of time with a bleating ram, and I sacrifice my son. I would have hurled myself out the window on the spot, except that the parlor is located on the ground floor and I would have suffered a few scratches and a bruise or two at best. So I faint, still gripping my howling offspring.

Next thing I know, I am lying flat on the floor, sniffing vinegar. "What happened?" I cry out when I come to, a drop of cognac dampening my lips.

"You fainted," my wife reveals, "my mother and I rushed to the rescue."

"All went well," Dr. B. reassures us, upon bandaging the wound and counseling on how to change the dressing. "Such bleeding is perfectly normal. And the father's reaction," he adds, "is not unusual."

All did indeed go well. I am pleased to report that my son and I took parallel leaks for years, as I had done with my dad, the arch of our simultaneous inundations spilling into the toilet bowl, until adolescent discretion put an end to such primordial male bonding rituals.

My son is a married man now, and may one day have a son of his own. But I will not advocate for a tribal flaying of the foreskin. The memory of his imagined mutilation still makes me break out in a cold sweat, not some rarefied philosophical Kierkegaardian fear and trembling, but a full-fledged, no-holds-barred bout of Jewish angst.

No cigars! Still, a shot of cognac would be nice.

The Spirit Tree

"The tree which moves some to tears of joy is in the eyes
of others only a green thing that stands in the way."

— William Blake

Rising, miraculous, precariously leaning in front of the attached one-family, red-brick, row house in which I grew up in Jackson Heights, Queens, in the time I lived there and for years thereafter, when my widowed mother was the sole remaining occupant, a towering fir tree loomed twice as tall as the roof and climbing. Having felled all extraneous timber and reduced their own allotted green space to a lifeless rectangle of cement, the neighbors to the right and left clamored for it to be cut down, complaining of the risk of its snapping in a storm, the nuisance of the fallen leaves in autumn, and the racket made by the birds it attracted. But my mother wouldn't hear of it. Living alone and fiercely independent, her attachment to the tree transcended insurance risk and real estate value.

A mere sapling when we first moved in, it went through astounding arboreal growth spurts, more than doubling every decade. I was in awe of its vitality. It grew tall as I stayed small, a magic beanstalk to my modulated Jack.

For my parents, who had fled their native Vienna, the tree conjured up romantic strolls in the idyllic Wienerwald of their youth. And though Jewish tradition precluded a Christmas Tree in the living room, come winter the sight of its green needles dusted white elicited an only partially ironic crooned chorus of "O, Tannenbaum!" from my wistful father and a smile from my grandmother who lived with us until her death at age 91. Hard of hearing, vision failing, uprooted as she was, she liked to sit at the window looking out on that abbreviated forest.

Though hardly blessed with green thumbs, and definitely not the gardening kind, my parents took a benevolent laissez faire attitude to nature, leaving weeds to grow wild, bushes to burgeon, and plants to proliferate front and rear. We had no pets, but among the vigorous green things that grew in our proximity was a stubborn shrub that my siblings and I dubbed "the jungle," on account of its ever-thickening trunk, prickly branches and dangling tendrils on which we longed to swing, Tarzan-style. And dare I forget the runty little fig tree, stunted and rendered sterile by countless frosts, or so we thought, till one day it fulfilled its botanical destiny, drooping with sweet figs!

In 1960, when I was eight, the howling gusts of Hurricane Donna wrought havoc, toppling great elms and telephone poles up and down the block, scattering them helter-skelter like so many giant pick-up sticks, forever dispelling any illusion of permanence. We feared for our fir, but though it swayed dangerously, branches snapping, needles shedding, the trunk held firm.

Once, in my later travels, I happened upon two seemingly identical kapok trees standing side-by-side at the edge of a village in the Casamance, in southern Senegal, the one lush, fluttering and twittering with birds, the other devoid of life. Were the leaves any larger, the worms any more succulent, or the shade any cooler on the one tree than on the other? I pointed out the seeming enigma to a wizened old animist who'd just shimmied up a nearby palm to tap its fermented sap for palm wine. The old man took a swig from his collecting bottle, before passing it to me, muttering matter-of-factly: "Spirit tree."

Respectfully skeptical at the time, I have since come to wonder.

Every morning for as long as she was able, my mother's first public act of the day after dressing and drinking her coffee, was to open the door and strew breadcrumbs saved from dinner the night before for the birds nesting in her beloved tree.

But following a nasty bout of pneumonia that sapped all her strength, she grew listless and immobile, rooted to the couch, ever more vegetative in manner.

"What about the birds?" we tried to rouse her, to no avail.

Call me a fool, but I believe the tree had a hand in her convalescence.

The long winter wound down with one last gust that whipped the mighty trunk about and made it rap with its wooden knuckles against the living room window. Roused out of her listless state, my mother remembered she had legs.

She was back at the door the next morning, strewing breadcrumbs for the birds, nodding at the tree, whose tilt had come to resemble her own.

Seven years after my mother's passing, my siblings and I finally brought ourselves to sell the house.

The new owners cut down the fir tree.

It's gone for good. But in the cemetery where my parents lie buried, rising out of a bed of ivy, an obstinate weed with a sturdy trunk, a dead ringer for a tree, spreads its branches overhanging their graves. The birds don't know the difference.

On Getting Older

To R.O.

A friend recently remarked: "I don't know how to get old." He meant it quite literally, referring to a life skill he felt he lacked, a tactic for navigating troubled waters.

"It's not a matter of getting old, but of getting older," I replied off the top of my head, without giving it a second thought.

The haphazard remark set off a train of thought I would quite frankly have preferred to, but could not, put out of my mind. What does it mean to get older? How well do I wear my years, or do I let them wear me out? My friend is ten years my junior and we have lived very different lives, but the challenge is essentially the same: whether to count backwards or forwards, or to use a hackneyed metaphor, to conceive of the glass half-full or half-empty.

My toenails, I notice, are taking on the erratic contour of a city skyline. My hairline is receding, eroding in visible patches, my short beard more salt than pepper. Eyes framed by sagging pockets above and below, brow furrowed with worry lines, the face is a reservoir of insult.

I am feeling a bit more brittle in my bones, more halting in my step, more hesitant of reflex. Time, I tell myself, is a two-way street. In the unguarded gaze of the aging, the infant peers forth, still young and hopeful, as yet unencumbered by the sediment of sadness and regret. And conversely, peeling the mask of innocence off the faces of children, you can excavate the visages of the ancients they will one day become. And so it goes, the boomeranging of skin and bone, of longings contained and distilled into the potent resin of regret.

Those of us born in the wake of World War II, the so-called Baby Boomers, and our heirs among the Millennials, were never weaned of Ponce de Leon's desperate thirst (delusive or visionary) for the fountain of eternal youth. Age, we believe, is a state of mind. "Ah, but I was so much older then, I'm younger than that now," sang Bob Dylan in his 1964 anthem to eternal youth "My Back Pages." It's not just an American thing. When once several years back, I bemoaned pushing 60, a French friend, already well into his eighties at the time, and in most respects a dire pessimist, put a rosy spin on it. "Sixty," he remarked with a wistful smile, "is the youth of old age."

But whereas until recently, past and future seemed to be about equally divided, my store of yesterdays has swelled somewhat of late and the prospective stock of tomorrows has definitely dwindled. Depending on my state of mind and a variety of affective factors, notably the response of others, in particular that of attractive young women, whether they engage my gaze or offer me their seat on the subway, thus reducing me to old-timer status, the consciousness of that tipping of the temporal scale either buoys my spirit or weighs me down, driving me on with a renewed burst of impatience to get things done, or causing me to dwell on — I won't say the word — call it the eventual cessation of the animate engine of will.

I have chucked a few useless illusions along the way and clung to, indeed fortified my faith in those I deem beneficial. So, for instance, I no longer crave acclaim as I once did.

Of course, I still want my writing to be read and recognized, but the measure of success has changed — I cherish meditative moments of lucidity and seek to draw them out, even now as I write this.

I feel at the top of my game when it comes to spinning sentences, which next to sex, remains my favorite activity. Come to think of it, in the absence of a wonder drug and sustained tantric prowess, writing promises a longer-lasting release.

In the past I wrote, at least in part, to draw attention to myself, like a peacock spreading his tail feathers. These days I write to tell time and situate myself in the moment. On the shelf before me, rows of notebooks weigh down the wood with the jottings of a half-century or so, most of interest only to myself. But at least I can flip through the pages, look back and confirm: I have lived, I have proof.

My father once confessed to me in an unguarded moment that the only way he managed to relieve his migraines and insomnia as a young man on the verge of middle age was to refrain from dreaming. I do not judge his decision. He lived through difficult times. The decision worked for him.

The sleepless grip has got me again. It is god knows what time. I can hear every creak in my bones, like the staircase of the house I grew up in, my father tramping down the steps to check on his shiftless son. The pencils rear up in a bucket on my writing table like spiked punk hair. I, now, seasoned paterfamilias of my own little clan, was about to make some grand declaration. I am feeling the ache of age, the itches, the stink, what I once called the potato-like smell of age.

My vitality has significantly diminished, the lion's share

gone for good. But the spirit in between the ears is still raging. The blood is singing an anthem, if only I knew the words and tune. Milking the udder of darkness while becoming dust, I keep peeling the skin of the moment, injecting a talking tattoo. I will keep at it till the ink runs dry.

The Third Line

On a recent visit to the aging aunt of a friend in a minuscule apartment crowded with plants in the Bronx, I was puzzled by her three telephones, two of which rang several times, as did her microwave, alarm clock, and various other tingling appurtenances — the pitch of each of which she was immediately able to tell apart, though given the profusion of vegetation, they sounded rather like exotic birdcalls.

"Why the three phones?" I asked after a while.

"One's for the folks I want to hear from, the other's for the ones I don't," she replied matter-of-factly.

"And the third?"

"The third," she said, "is for the unexpected."

"But it never rings!"

"If it did," she shrugged, "it'd stop being unexpected."

Nodding politely, an involuntary twitch of my right eyebrow bespoke my bafflement, whereupon she told me the following story.

"Years ago," she began, "I got this lump in my throat the size of a walnut that wouldn't go away. With two young boys at home, I couldn't afford to fall ill. Seated in the waiting room at the hospital, I worried myself sick, expecting the worst, when an unfamiliar bell rang. I turned around in time to see an elevator door open and a very pale-looking young nun step out. Not 'n ordained nun, but a novitiate, you know, the kind that hadn't yet taken her vows, all dressed in white.

Her face was as white as her habit.

"Seeing how distressed I looked, she comes directly over to me. 'Why're you so worried, dear?' she asks.

"I burst out crying.

"'I'll pray for you,' she says, 'n puts her hand on my neck. "Deliver us from evil: For thine is the kingdom, and the power and the glory," she prayed. I wa'n't a believer back then, but not wanting to offend, I just nodded. 'Call if you need to talk,' she said, handing me a card.

"It was a long and arduous treatment. After every chemo I heaved my guts out on the sidewalk. The radiation burnt my hair out. Still, in time I got better. My hair grew back, but thank God, the cancer didn't. Rummaging around in my pocketbook one day, I found the card. Maybe the prayers helped, maybe not! I wanted to thank her, so I dialed the number. An unfamiliar area code, I figured it must be a convent someplace upstate. It rang and rang with a funny faraway echo. I was about to hang up, when, finally, somebody picks up. — 'Can I speak to Sister Mary Immaculate, please?' I ask.

"Silence on the other end of the line.

"'Does Sister Mary still live there?' I pressed.

"'My daughter, Mary Ellen, died ten years ago, God rest her soul,' says a deeply distraught woman's voice. 'She was about to take her vows.'

"'That's not possible,' I protested. 'I saw her with my own eyes step out of an elevator and walk toward me nine months ago at Misericordia Hospital. Maybe they changed the name o' the place.'

"'That's where she died, throat cancer,' the mother replied all choked up. 'Never smoked a cigarette.'

"'I'm so sorry,' I said.

The line went silent.

"I got me another two phone lines over the years, for the reason I explained, but still keep the third just in case.

Just then a bell rang with an unfamiliar ring.

She let it ring three, four, five, maybe seven times, until I could no longer bear the anticipation.

"Which telephone is it?" I asked.

"It's the doorbell," she said. "I'm expecting a delivery."

Rough Cuts

I

Today the surgeon cut a little cancer out of me. A parcel of self that had grown wild and threatened to consume the rest. Hair has that tendency too if left to its own devices. Barber and surgeon are historically related at the root. Only the instruments have changed. Cut it out! you insist, cancer is no laughing matter. Cancer kills you if you don't uproot it. It's a kind of shoot-out at the O.K. Corral, the surgeon a high-paid gunslinger, or rather knife wielder, hired to have it out with my renegade cells.

Now this particular cancer happened to grow on my right forearm, a nasty place for any right-handed person, all the more so for a writer.

"Easy does it, nothing to it," remarked the surgeon with a certain swagger no doubt meant to reassure the patient. "If you had to pick a cancer from a catalogue, that's the one you'd want."

Comforted somewhat that the surgeon approved of my choice, I opted for a local anesthetic, wanting to have my wits about me during the procedure.

While cutting, the surgeon kept us both entertained with a wry account of a patient he'd once operated on at Bellevue, a drunk who'd lost a leg after stumbling in between a colliding truck and a taxi, in an accident in which the taxi driver also lost a leg. The drunk's no less inebriated buddies sent him directly to the hospital in an ambulance and dutifully followed in a cab, clutching the severed limb which they'd managed to salvage from the wreckage before the crashed vehicles burst into flames. Only when they got to the hospital, the surgeon pointed out to them that they'd plucked the wrong leg out of the wreckage, and that, henceforth, their friend would hobble through life on two left legs.

Apocryphal perhaps, the story lasted as long as the cutting. "I just love to cut!" the surgeon shook his head with a wistful sigh, evidently disappointed that it was already over and done with.

I myself was relieved. "If you had to pick a talent from the catalogue," I said, "that's the one I'd want you to have!"

For the stitching, he told me of an old Village character, a poet with no health insurance, who paid for each operation with a poem. "I remember one about a pair of surgical scissors, but don't ask me to recite it," he said, "mnemonics is not one of my strengths."

"I'm from The Village too," I said.

"No poems, please," he said, "you pay."

Fortunately, I had insurance. My only regret was not to have taken a parting glimpse at the piece of me he cut out.

In a grudging way I admired the cancer for its stubborn will to grow, its total lack of concern for the surrounding cells comprising the rest of me. If only we could harness such pig-headed resolve to grow parts of ourselves on demand. In my case, I wouldn't mind adding an inch or two at the top and trimming the same round the middle. From Nature's perspective, I suppose, humanity is one big hungry tumor growing wildly beyond its allotted slot, colonizing, conquering, consuming.

Think I'll go get a haircut.

2

Staring down at the heap of fleece on the floor after a haircut, I have always suffered a pang of separation as if from a disposable accumulation of self. And when lifting what's left of me out of the barber chair, I wobble a bit, feeling out the lightness and the loss.

Haircuts have always been traumatic.

Once, while I was in the hot seat at the barbershop in my early boyhood, a black limousine pulled up and a man with a black Fedora stepped out. Not ordinarily given to undue haste, Giuseppe, who had just about finished my right side, ran to hold the door. "A trim," said the man, removing his Fedora, revealing a more or less bald pate with a white fuzz round the ears. Making a big to-do over every strand, Giuseppe kept trembling after the man had gone. My mother had to remind him to attend to the left side of my head.

In late adolescence, I tried a barber school. With their hair slicked back and glittering gold teeth, the barbers-in-training looked like hungry young sharks, but once having entered their precinct I was too intimidated to contemplate escape. Nodding at my request for a parting on the left, my trainee, who had been trimming his nose hairs, reached for an electric sheer and proceeded to take it all off, military-style. "What about the parting?" I asked, straining to hold back the tears. He shook his head and shrugged: "Too short!"

There were those years, following the arrival of the Beatles, when having it cut meant capitulation to the fleece police. Lean years for the trade.

Various girlfriends subsequently had a go at it, but the Samson and Delilah thing and a few mishaps prompted me to return to professionals.

Vincent, my current cutter, likes to talk about the plot of land he owns in Upstate New York. He can close his eyes, he claims, and picture every wild flower and weed. I figure a man who respects things that grow will go easy on the wispy boundary between being and nothingness.

Conversing with my reflection in the mirror — as tenuous a part of me as the falling locks — Vincent tells tales of the trade: what hairdos Madonna, an erstwhile client, used to have done before she made it, and how the late playwright Miguel Piñero dropped by one day before presenting his first script to the late impresario Joseph Papp. "Lighten me up for luck!" he said. Papp took the play and put Piñero on the map. Vincent has not yet performed such miracles for me, but I'm a patient man and consider each haircut a high-risk investment.

On Losing the Use of my Nose

It suddenly dawned on me one day, hitting me square in the nose, that for quite some time now, just how long I could not say, I have had no sense of smell.

An absence, particularly the absence of one of the five senses, a fundamental element of life you had always taken for granted, is more difficult to detect than a presence.

What's missing? You wonder, unable to pinpoint just what it is. Has some practical joker gone and painted the sky a different color when you weren't looking? No, the sky is still the same mottled blue. Your fingers and toes still grasp the palpable borderline between self and other. The incessant cacophony of traffic confirms that your ears still work fine. You can still taste the food on your plate, but something in your apperception of the palette of flavors is awry. Then it dawns on you by elimination. It's your nose that's out of whack. Only it isn't allergy season, there's no cat in sight, and you don't have a cold.

I had always been particularly attentive to smells, my own and that of others. Since early childhood I had taken to sniffing my own left wrist in the morning upon waking and at odd moments during the day to confirm my existence: I smell myself, therefore I am. And then, of course, there was the smell of my amassed bodily filth before bathing, with which I was both initially reticent and later relieved to part.

There is the smell of friends and family members, each with his or her own unmistakable register. And the enthralling, nose-tingling smell of intimacy, when first you burst out of the bubble of self and risk proximity with another — each subsequent contact being an olfactory explosion, those that smell good and those that do not.

The nose knows. It has long been considered a kind of Geiger counter and lightning rod. To have a nose for something signifies a natural ability. Conversely, a red nose is a dead giveaway for a drunk. Pinocchio's nose grows when he tells lies, a metaphoric counterpart to that other body part that swells at the most inappropriate moments. Are we not all old dogs at heart, or rather at nose, our olfactory capacity diminished by standing upright, repeated bathing, and dabs of deodorant, but ever craving that long-lost proximity to the posteriors of our fellow creatures! Is not smell still the most potent trigger of memory, peeling away years in an instant!

I remember the immediate effect of one scent, in particular. It came from a scratch ad in a magazine, a musky fragrance then newly released by a leading French perfumer. My wife and I were propped up side by side, reading in bed. I tore off and dabbed the crushed pellet strip on her shoulder blade. Even now my nostrils twitch and hormones well up at the memory, though I can no longer smell it.

How can I convey the sense of loss!? A dimension has vanished forever and life is less rich for it, as if a primary color disappeared from the palette of experience. I try to comfort myself at the thought that blindness and deafness are so much more debilitating, and if one of the five senses had to go, better it be that.

I would like to think that I'm not entirely nose-blind, but rather suffering from a kind of "near-nosedness." I do, on occasion, revel in a faint whiff on the street or standing beside someone in an elevator, but can never be quite certain that it's not my mind playing tricks on me.

Passion is a curious customer and memory the most potent stimulant. I still ask my wife to put on the same perfume, and imagine, or rather, nose-up the effect of that trace of a fragrance buried in my brain, prodding the old dog to dig it up like a bone. The sense distilled into its essence, whether it's the scent or its reverberating absence, a pheromone trigger or an olfactory hallucination, it still does the trick.

To Sleep, Perchance to Dream

In childhood, sleep loomed as an irksome intrusion, a punishment imposed by grownups to reign in and tame the little wildcats in their charge. The prospect of bedtime pulled the plug on the boundless pleasure of play, which is all I really lived for. Nothing bothered me more than being sent to bed, and worst of all, for a nap smack dab in the middle of the day. Dreams offered a modicum of delight, a vivid consolation for the requisite forty winks.

But as I round out my sixth decade of life, finally retired from the daily grind of gainful employment, free at last to indulge all my whimsies, notably to engage in wordplay, my chosen form of amusement, the imp of the perverse goes and pulls a fast one. Ironically, now that I call the shots, chronic insomnia causes near constant fatigue, and I crave sleep wherever and whenever I can get it.

The ancient Greeks pictured Hypnos, the son of Nyx (the Night) and Erebus (the Darkness), and twin brother of Thanatos (Death), as the personification of Sleep. Hypnos resides in a deep dark cave, out of which the river Lethe (Forgetfulness) flows, and at the mouth of which sprout poppies and other hypnotic flora. Not a ray of light, nor a shred of sound ever seeps into his grotto on the isle of Lemnos, the remote locus of reverie. In contrast to the nasty pranks pulled by his fellow deities, the benevolent god of sleep is said to help mortals find release, in exchange for which they gratefully sacrifice to him half of their lives. These days, however, Hypnos appears to withhold his gifts.

Throughout much of my life I needed to log in a good eight to ten hours of sleep at a stretch to function at my best. Age has definitely altered the balance. I have in recent years resorted to various pills, salves and tinctures to hasten shut-eye. But I am beginning to think that it is a mistake to force the issue. Perhaps I now need to scatter sleep, or rather to alternate somnolence and lucidity, spreading them evenly throughout the day. Notwithstanding the Protestant work ethic, with which we Americans are inculcated, whatever our faith or the lack thereof, there is something particularly enticing about the prospect of a secret tryst with the unconscious. Though frowned upon by the stiff-upper-lip leanings of Anglo-Saxon culture — Hamlet's oft-quoted line "to sleep, perchance to dream," was, after all, uttered while contemplating suicide — elsewhere, adult napping is the norm.

As luck would have it, I married into a southern French farming family, for which *la sieste* is a quasi-sacred rite zealously practiced by all the males. My late father-in-law withdrew daily for his hour of shut-eye after lunch. My wife recalls that on summer trips and extended family outings, when fatigue hit, he would pull the car over, lay his head on the steering wheel, and zone out for a quarter of an hour or so to recharge the psychic battery.

With the cannons of war booming nearby, another Frenchman, Napoleon Bonaparte, retired to his imperial tent for a short catnap before returning to the front to lead his men into battle. Of course, Napoleon lost out in the end. And who is to say that a greater vigilance and a more regular sleep regimen might not ultimately have averted his defeat at the hands of the Duke of Wellington!

But Winston Churchill, another Brit of note, also took

midday naps to maintain his stamina, and he won the war.

The diverse brotherhood of maverick nappers includes the likes of Leonardo da Vinci, Thomas Alva Edison, Albert Einstein, and John F. Kennedy. But high performing homo sapiens are not alone in this regard. Plants, animals, fungi and bacteria, it turns out, all self-regulate according to circadian rhythms, switching on and off based on certain chronobiological imperatives.

It is 1:45 PM of a gray December afternoon. Eyelids drooping, I halfheartedly fight off fatigue. As the French put it so poetically, *je n'ai pas les yeux en face des trous* (my eyes are not aligned with the lids.) And even as I try to string these words together and strain to make sense, Hypnos beckons like a wily sphinx.

Catch you later, dear reader! Pleasant dreams!

II

Fun and Games

On the Need to Waste Time Before Undertaking a Serious Task

Consider it a sacrifice to the divine god(dess) of sloth, an affirmation of free will, indeed a veritable hallmark of humanity — as opposed to the dogged drive to forage for food, defend against attack, procreate or poop. Never mind the old bugbear about time and money. Life is neither a ledger sheet nor a balanced bank account. Wasting time, i.e. doing whatever you damn well please in an aimless, unfocused fashion, not only relaxes the spirit, it simultaneously dissipates tension and revs up the synaptic sparks of concentration in preparation for the task at hand.

Let us begin by establishing a fundamental premise: No two time-spans are alike, even if the ticking thing that chops up eternity into temporal units presupposes equivalence. Our experience, for instance, of a heart-racing, sweat-soaked rush of rapture on the edge of jouissance is fundamentally different from the same stretch of time spent waiting, the former of lightning-like velocity and exquisite intensity, the latter of an unendurably tedious, snail-like crawl. And even the perceived quality of waiting time depends on what you're waiting for. Waiting, say, for a fine meal to be served, your mouth watering, nostrils tingling with the scents emanating from the kitchen, bears little, if any, resemblance to the boredom of a bout of waiting at a bus stop, or an equi-temporal spell of anticipatory pain in advance of the dentist's drill.

Sometimes, of course, entrenched in the pursuit of whatever whimsy you're engaged in, you lose track of time and never get down to business. So be it. The whimsy won out and the business will just have to wait.

Among the most delightful moments in life is that infinitesimal juncture between twilight and dusk at the tail end of a weekday, as darkness closes in. Having succeeded or failed to accomplish your goal, you temporarily suspend the compulsion to pursue purposeful action, and simply exist, allowing yourself, as they say, to "call it a day." Complete indulgence calls for a glass of something to mark the moment. It is then, ironically enough, with the pressure off, that you often come up with your best ideas.

*

Such heavenly hiatuses can, of course, occur by happenstance or choice in any place at any time. I remember with a sentiment akin to sacred reverence that moment, mid-afternoon, well into a seemingly interminable spell of waiting for a connecting flight at the Marco Polo Airport outside Venice, when fed-up glancing back and forth between my wristwatch and an electronic timetable of delayed departures on the far wall, espying a bar near at hand, I decided to submit to a passing whim and order a glass of Amarone, the velvety rich, red local elixir made from dried grapes on the verge of becoming raisins, actually grown in the vineyards of the nearby Province of Verona. There was something in that first sip that instantly metamorphosed the torment of anticipation into an exquisite foretaste of eternity. Suddenly, time no longer mattered, or rather, it felt like I was riding it as a surfer rides an ocean wave. And when, at last, the timetable announced the impending departure and gate, I had to force myself to rise along with the rest, almost disappointed to be going anywhere other than where I already was.

A Forgotten Game

I don't know who invented the game or whether it is still played today. Slap Ball had a brief vogue in New York City schoolyards in the early Sixties, and in Jackson Heights, Queens, where I grew up, it attained minor cult status as the game of choice for the physically inept. A welcome alternative to punch ball, softball, and baseball, in which I performed so poorly the other kids would crowd around snickering when I got up to bat, waiting for me to strike out — slap ball was my chance to shine.

A game of extreme constraint, played in the tight confines of a handball court with the diamond grid of the ballpark chalked in miniature on the buckled cement, it demanded more cunning than real skill, more spryness than hand-eye coordination, more gumption than athletic prowess.

As an aphorism is to an epic, so slap ball shrank the expectations of the ballpark to bite-sized proportions. For whereas the vast sweep of the playing field ringed with onlookers had always seemed intimidating, invariably bringing on bowed shoulders of defeat and an asthmatic wheeze, its microcosmic equivalent squeezed into the confines of an outdoor handball court felt strangely comforting. It was as if the safe haven of my childhood nursery had been lifted, walls and all, from home and plunked down in a distant corner of the schoolyard where nobody noticed it. That precisely was the game's greatest attraction and its greatest fault: that nobody noticed.

Slap ball victories were won way off the radar of public approbation, and any attempt to boast about them would have been met with blank looks.

But I can still recall the day in sixth grade when a few of the same champions, gruff Kenny P., tall Mark R., glib Gary S., and my nemesis Robert H., not a one of whom would ever in the grand public sphere of the spectacle have deigned to choose me for their team, stood there holding their ground with meager expectations, when somebody pitched. Bluffing with a grin at Gary S. and a wink at Robert H., I swung with the flat palm of my hand, putting a devilish spin on the red rubber ball so that it went careening, almost perpendicular to my slap, in between the legs of a disconcerted Kenny P, grazed the crack at the chalk baseline near third base, and bounced toward a rattled Mark R., who fumbled with and dropped it, while Robert H.'s jaw dropped, permitting me ample time to round the bases and make my way to home plate.

They stared at me as if I had just stepped out of my loser's skin and revealed a hidden side of myself, like the bespectacled Clark Kent morphing into Superman, or the wimpy Peter Parker into the spry Spider-Man, a local Queens-born hero who had recently made his first appearance in the pages of Amazing Fantasy. Just this once I might have earned bragging rights, were it not for the news report from Dallas.

It was just after the start of recess, approximately 11:35 Eastern Time, Friday, November 22, 1963. The teachers suddenly called us into the auditorium for an unexpected assembly, at which the principal announced in a solemn voice that the president had been shot, simultaneously perhaps also the death blow for slap ball, and we were dismissed for the day. Expecting adulation, I could barely choke back my disappointment. Dallas seemed as far away as the moon. All everybody really cared about was the half day off from school.

The Sultry Scent of Formaldehyde

> "Humor can be dissected, as a frog can, but the thing
> dies in the process and the innards are discouraging
> to any but the purely scientific mind."
>
> —E.B. White

My memories of high school are burdened by two deciding factors: the absence of girls and my aversion to math and science, both regrettable, given the fact that the prestigious institution I attended, Stuyvesant High School — then still in its old digs, a venerable building on East 15th Street slowly sinking into the quicksand of the past — was all-boys and all about math and science.

Numbers make me nervous.

Our chemistry teacher, Mr. L., word has it, the erstwhile proprietor of a failed soap factory, manages to drain the periodic table of any pizazz, except for when he divides water into its component parts and makes the hydrogen pop with a match.

Physics is far too abstract.

Algebra, forget about it.

Geometry, taught by a certain Mr. S., is slightly less odious, since it involves spinning narratives with numbers, describing the nature of spaces and magnitudes.

Playing hooky from school one day at lunchtime, I dodge into a nearby cinema. They're showing the movie *Ulysses*, based on the novel by James Joyce, which I mistakenly conflate with *Lady Chatterley's Lover*, by D.H. Lawrence, both not on our English reading list, the racy passages of the latter pondered at night under the covers. I am the only spectator in the entire theater, and honestly, I don't remember much, except for the bushy eyebrows of Leopold Bloom wiggling when he gets excited. I study the screen from every seat in the house, attempting to calibrate the hypotenuse of my adolescent dismay, largely oblivious to the young hero Stephen Daedalus' Jesuit, heavily Irish-accented musings in the course of his perambulations around Dublin, a locale that seems infinitely far removed from my Jewish-inflected New York. But I am gripped by his love interest, the sultry Molly Bloom, lying in bed, getting all worked up over a run-on sentence that never would have washed in English class: "so he could feel my breasts all perfume yes and his heart going like mad and yes I said yes I will Yes."

She brings to mind my biology teacher, who has a way of tossing back her hair to make a point, seated cross-legged on her desk, baring her knees — her name escapes me now. For her I would have done anything. For her I even resolve to do well in biology.

As part of our midterm grade, we are to be tested on our capacity to dissect and identify the inner organs of a frog. In preparation, I kidnap one from the lab, sedate it with formaldehyde, and take it home in a pickle jar with holes punctured in the lid to let it breathe.

On the subway ride back to Queens, as we pass under the East River and I feel the pop in my ear, a factor linked to the change in water pressure, as we'd learned in class, my heart throbbing for Miss X, I unscrew and lift the lid to confirm that the frog is still alive. But the sedative must have worn off. The moment I peak in, he leaps out and a chorus of shrieks accompany his zigzagging peregrinations around the subway car.

I finally recover my subject. And though my makeshift sedative of vinegar, mercurochrome and apricot brandy doesn't quite do the trick, and his little legs wiggle like Leopold Bloom's eyebrows under the knife, I manage to extract and identify each part, setting aside the heart.

At our graded dissection the next day, to the amazement of my teacher, I excise, pin down and identify 11 out of a possible 10 organs. (It is the only time math and science ever work in my favor.) Convinced that I had stumbled on a rare mutation, a frog with two hearts, she broadcasts the finding throughout the school, and I briefly bask in the glow of my grade of A+. My dissection is left on display in the glass case outside the biology lab until the organs rot.

The school admits girls in 1969, the fall after I graduate.

A lot of good it did me.

How the French Test their Mettle

Like the chirp of the cicada, the clink of steel on steel is a signal sound of the south of France. "Ooh la!" they cry when a deft *tireur* (or "shooter") lands a *carreau*, a perfect pitch, knocking an opponent's boule out of the way and dropping his own in its place. "*Il a le biais!*" (He's got the toss!) they declare and toast his prowess with a cool pastis.

But the game of boules is not limited to the Midi. As French as the baguette, it is played with equal passion, albeit by different rules and with projectiles of various shapes and sizes, on rough and smooth terrains all over France, and can indeed be said to be the national pastime.

Each version has its own pitch and flavor. There are the indoor games, like the flattened *boule de fort* preferred in Tours, and the big round *boule de Nantes* tossed on a curved wooden court. The Bretons play *la boule bretonne* with hard wood balls and celebrate with cider. In the northeastern variant, *boule de Flandre*, they hurl a metallic disc and clink victory over beer. But by far the most popular versions, *le jeu lyonnais* from Lyon, *le jeu provençal* and its offshoot, *la pétanque*, both originally from Provence, are now played everywhere.

Boules has been traced back to the ancient Greeks, who hurled round stones, and the Romans, who pitched wooden balls wrapped in iron. Rusty archeological specimens have been dug up in Marseille.

The oldest documented version of the game, *la lyonnaise*, also known as *la longue* (the long game), was first played in the 18th century in the city of Lyon and its surroundings. The rules were codified in 1850. The boules are larger and heavier than those employed in *le jeu provençal* and *la pétanque*, and players take a prescribed three-steps to hurl. *La lyonnaise* has of late gained a global following as a serious sport. In addition to the French, teams from six other nations—Italy, Bosnia and Herzegovina, Monaco, Slovenia, Croatia, and China—have competed most summers at the lovely tree-lined *boulodrome* of the Grand Prix de Gap (Hautes-Alpes). And though the French team from Lyon took home the trophy, the Chinese offered stiff opposition, earning the crowd's respect and raising hopes of one day taking the game to the Olympics.

In Provence, they prefer a considerably less strenuous version called *la pétanque* (literally *pieds tanqués*, or anchored feet), equally prized by nonagenarians like the late singer Henri Salvador, stocky Marseille dockworkers, fishermen, farmhands, bankers in business suits, and bathing beauties in bikinis. *La pétanque* was reputedly invented in 1907 in La Ciotat (a port just outside Marseille) by a certain Jules (aka "Tonin") le Noir, a player well past his prime who suffered from rheumatism, and so, refused to budge.

You just crouch, aim, and pitch. With the palm faced down and a little practice you can put a backspin on your boule to make it stop short. In fact, it's more like horse-shoes than bowling, a toss rather than a roll. A century after its creation, the game's popularity has soared as the leisure activity of choice from the shady Place des Lices in St.-Tropez and Marseille's Parc Borély to the Place de la Nation in Paris, and every autoroute rest stop and village square in between.

Like pool in America, *la pétanque* is both an amateurs' passion indulged for fun and a calculated hustle played for high stakes. In either case it is no laughing matter, and like every game worth playing, a test of one's mettle and a lesson for life.

I was coached in one memorable match some years ago by my late father-in-law, a retired physics teacher, in the tiny Alpine village of Les Savoyons, in the Hautes-Alpes, where he was born. The object is to place your boules closest to the little wooden jack, called a *cochonnet* (literally, piglet), and scatter those of your opponent. There are two essential skills involved, to *pointe* (or place) your boule, and to *tire* (or shoot), displacing the competition. I was lobbing and hurling with careless abandon, invariably missing my mark. "Why don't you aim?!" my father-in-law frowned. It had never occurred to me that I could. Then to everyone's utter amazement, not least of all my own, I did just that, and pulled off a perfect *carreau*. Lord, what a lovely clink! Revelations are seldom so simple and sweet.

On Ironing a Shirt

Pressing down hard with the hot iron set to steam mode on the wrinkled cotton of a shirt fished fresh out of the washing machine, the launderer is afforded the ability to impress a satisfying smoothness on the chaos of life. All day long, flung hither and thither, seemingly at the mercy of the whims of fate, life feels largely out of my hands, but come evening, once a week, on ironing night I have the power to impress my will. It is no doubt something of an exaggeration, but to that determined hand holding down the iron, the shirt stretched out before me on the ironing board is not just a shirt, but a metaphor with magical import practically akin to that of the sacramental host to the lips of the believer. The import in my case is, in fact, more Animist than Catholic. The collar, shirt sleeves, and rear neck pleat approximate a limp body, a kind of headless voodoo doll, which, like a divine masseur, I ply into shape.

The ironing board is my altar. The ritual ironing order is always the same.

I begin by pressing down on the collar, vicariously feeling the heat around my own neck, making me stand up a little straighter. The front folds surgically incised and divided down chest and belly come next, first the right side bearing the line of buttons, the hot iron symbolically straightening out the wrinkled skin around a row of plastic umbilici, then the side with the slits. At this stage I am an obstetrician, or rather a midwife, pulling the wriggling thing out of the washing machine womb, dangling it upside-down, as it were, slapping life into the pliant material.

The left breast pocket demands particular attention as the symbolic lid over the heart.

Now I turn to the sleeves, starting with the cuffs, generally the left cuff first, though this is not a hard and fast rule, and sometimes the right cuff beckons. Only thereafter does the hot iron slide down the length of each sleeve. Spread out on the board, the sleeves undergo a benign crucifixion preceding the shirt's apotheosis. The image may sound a bit extreme, no blood being spilt, no pain inflicted, and perhaps a soothing shiatsu massage is more apt, stretching the prone voodoo symbol of self.

Finally, I flip over the flattened effigy and turn my attention to the back, beginning with the rear neck pleat running down the line of the spine, careful to preserve its discreet contour. A neck pleat fold out of place can wreak virtual havoc with the posture of the wearer. I confess that at this point, my attention to detail slackens somewhat, particularly after ironing a rack of shirts, and I may leave an unconscionable wrinkle just above the coccyx, where once an ancestral tail wagged.

Laundering and ironing were in the past the exclusive domain of launderesses, working class women accorded little social prestige. French novelist Émile Zola dramatized their hapless lot in his novel *L'Assommoir*. The situation changed a little with the advent of the electric iron. Yet the task still essentially fell to women, the housewife being charged with keeping her husband's shirts starched and ironed.

But with the Women's Liberation Movement and its concomitant liberating effects on men, roles have shifted and tasks have loosened from their heretofore hard and fast gender assignment. Like other middle-class males of my generation, I have ventured into the kitchen and staked claim to the hearth as the designated cook in the family. Averse to messes, my wife remains the maven and mistress of orderliness in the house, the straightener-upper of the family — except for when it comes to ironing.

I am not alone among men in my affinity for this task. I have heard of a recent trend among male business executives, particularly in Great Britain, but also in the US, to iron their own shirts as a meditative, stress-busting mode of relaxation. According to a posting I read on the website *i-News, The Essential Daily Briefing*, the Hilton Garden Inn Heathrow, outside London, has launched an Ironing Club, with attendees participating in a 30-minute session led by a relaxation expert.

I would not go to such lengths to unwind, and prefer to iron alone at night in the confines of my own home, with a shot of single malt whiskey close at hand to iron out the internal wrinkles that the iron missed.

The Importance of Getting Goofy

"Pay attention to your nonsense."

—Ludwig Wittgenstein

I have a fatherly confession to make. I've never read *The Seven Secrets of Effective Fathers* or *The Five Key Habits of Smart Dads*, and am not now, nor have I ever been, or plan to become a card-carrying member of the National Center for Fathering, the National Fatherhood Initiative or the Promise Keepers. I learned the essentials of fathering from my father, who for devotion and affection was a pretty tough act to follow. The most important thing he ever taught me, aside from tying my shoelaces and the facts of life, was how to turn the world on its head and see things upside down and inside out.

Nonsense! you say.

Precisely!

Forget all the experts' solemn hype! Too much earnestness is lethal, bad for the blood pressure, your batting average, and every other function linked to the human heart.

Get goofy!

My father was by no means a frivolous man. An old-fashioned educator to the bone who drilled me in French irregular verbs, Latin declensions and logarithms for fun, he interspersed his lessons with generous helpings of foolishness, conceptual sugar to help the medicine go down. So, for instance, if he lost his temper and tweaked or buffeted me gently, as he sometimes did to reel in my wandering mind, I was licensed to reply with a stroke of my pen on his bare belly, which, incidentally, he referred to as his "fried chicken cemetery" in loving memory of all the succulent pullets there laid to rest. An unorthodox pedagogical method perhaps, it did permanently affix French irregular verbs to my funny bone and ensure that in later life I could hold my own with any surly concierge or insolent waiter.

Life's most important lessons are not necessarily limited to the strictly utilitarian. While physical fitness was definitely not my father's forte, he did instruct me in one astounding and spiritually restorative stunt, which I, in turn, have passed on to my children. Tilting toward each other, partners execute a perfect forehead-to-forehead 360-degree turn, twice in unison, first clockwise and then counterclockwise, to insure a proper sense of balance. Try it sometime with your offspring or spouse at a moment of conflict! While it may not make you see eye-to-eye, the synchronized concerted effort levels off differences, which is at least a step in the right direction.

I, for my part, taught my children when they were little just how to wind themselves up each morning by the nose, though my son took a while to get the hang of it and tended for the longest time to mistake his proboscis for a battering ram and mine for a spare pacifier. I revealed to him the location of the secret tongue-release button under the chin and demonstrated how to steer it with either ear, more arcane wisdom passed down from my Dad that never failed to send my son into peals of laughter.

On countless occasions I cautioned my daughter against the rude habit of treading on her shadow's toes. "How would you like it," I said, "if it stepped on yours!?" And I instructed her in the Zen art of walking between the drops on rainy days, though at best, I'm afraid, she only managed to elude every other drop.

What good did all this nonsense do them? you ask. Did it endear my children to their teachers? I doubt it. Boost their IQ up a notch? Not likely. Improve their performance on standardized exams and help get them into a top college, from thence into law school and, thereafter, insure their future prosperity? I can't say it helped them succeed in life.

But nonsense is a sound investment and an inoculation against gloom. For richer or for poorer, in sickness and in health, it may just have made them happier people better equipped to weather adversity and stress.

You still want proof?

I could cite a Harvard study about the benefits of humor as an effective coping mechanism, but that would be too stodgy.

Come to think of it, I did once put the art of the ridiculous to practical use. As an undergraduate scheduled to be interviewed by a committee of professors for a highly prized fellowship, I was nervously pacing up and down before the closed door, waiting my turn, worrying about what I would be asked and how I would reply intelligently. Then the door flew open, my name was called, and my heart started racing. Forgetting everything I had ever learned my mind went blank as I stumbled over the threshold and managed by some unfortunate fluke to get the heel of my shoe caught on a protruding nail. I yanked at it and, horror of horrors, the heel came off. With all eyes upon me, on the verge of tears, I wanted to turn and run. Instead, falling back on my father's wisdom, I bent down, picked up the heel, and purposefully limping, Charlie Chaplin's Little Tramp-style, took my seat. Setting the heel on the table before me, I remarked: "I see you set booby traps for your applicants!"

The solemn professors who had been sifting through applications and grilling applicants all day long exploded in laughter. Needless to say, I had that fellowship in the bag. I would have coached them all in Dad's 360-degree equilibrium-engendering turn, but figured I'd better stop while I was ahead.

In Defense of Fertile Clutter

"If a cluttered desk is a sign of a cluttered mind,
of what, then, is an empty desk a sign?"

Remark attributed to Albert Einstein

Marie Kondo, the popular, sylphlike, Japanese organizing guru and lifestyle expert, whose books have sold millions, recommends you limit your own private book collection to 30 volumes max. That might well work for a collection of haikus. But I must confess that my holdings currently surpass her recommendation by several hundredfold, including the leaning tower of Pisa of the books I'm currently reading, heaped on my night table.

"Dirt is essentially disorder," writes anthropologist Mary Douglas in her classic work *Purity and Danger*. Douglas is decidedly less judgmental. "There is no such thing as absolute dirt," she concedes, "it exists in the eye of the beholder!" I for my part am absolutely beholden to what some may deem my disorder, but which I would rather designate as my gold mine.

I have oftentimes gone digging in my walled stash of books, scanning the spines, and stumbled upon a title I did not know I had, but which proved particularly appropriate to the moment. The discovery, for instance, of Daniel Defoe's *Journal of the Plague Year*, a dusty, dog-eared copy of which I plucked like a ripe fruit off my shelf, offered the titillation of a horror flick in its precise description of past sufferings, coupled with vicarious comfort in the knowledge that the protagonist did, after all, live to tell the tale, and so, by example, fortified me with the faith that, walled in by my books, I, too, might survive covid-19, the dreaded plague of the moment. Of course, I could've downloaded Defoe off the internet, but I would first have had to know what I was looking for, and onscreen reading strains the eyes. I could've found it in the library, but here too would've forfeited the pleasure of haphazard discovery, and libraries are in any case closed at the moment.

One's own books, furthermore, a bit like one's own body smell, have a private appeal, stained as they are with tea and coffee spills and blanketed in the dust of time. I shamelessly admit to the vile habit of scribbling in the margins of my books — they are mine, after all, to do with as I see fit — and derive great pleasure years after the fact in reconsidering the passages I underlined, or as in the case of my disintegrating copy of James Joyce's *Ulysses*, in deciphering the hieroglyphs of my student doodles.

Am I indifferent to disorder? No, I'm just differently disposed to it.

Stacks of papers rise like miniature stalagmites from the bare parquet floor of my home office, beside unpaid bills, unanswered letters, chairs that wobble, watches that mercifully tell attenuated time, and various pieces of equipment that might or might not function if I ever forced the issue. Unnavigable to the untrained eye, I alone know where everything goes, and like it that way.

Most men of my acquaintance have a garage or workshop, attic, atelier or shed, a secret clubhouse heaped with dubious treasures precious to none but themselves, a cave in which to hibernate and brood, a semi-sacred precinct of privacy, strictly off limits to vacuum cleaner and broom. White collar, blue collar, or collarless tee-shirted, we're all still Tom Sawyers at heart, escaping from Aunt Polly's organizational talons. In our wayward ways, disorder liberates and dirt is a cleansing thing.

So, please, Marie Kondo, keep your fingers out of my mess.

III

Epiphanies of the Palate

"Your body is not a temple, it's an amusement park. Enjoy the ride."
— Anthony Bourdain

Epiphanies of the Palate

Marcel Proust wrote his 4,215-page-long novel, *À la Recherche du Temps Perdu*, sparked by the remembered taste of a tiny Madeleine biscuit. A comparative assessment of fish and clam chowders kicks off Herman Melville's seafaring saga *Moby Dick*. Asked upon his return to the U.S. after many years' absence what he missed most about the States, the émigré American author Paul Bowles, best known for his vivid evocations of North Africa, replied without hesitation: "Cherry Jell-O!"

The recollection of certain tastes can stir the soul to silent rapture.

I, too, keep a mental log.

Like the new potatoes picked up at a roadside stand in rural Maine, boiled on the hotplate of a motel kitchenette, dabbed with butter, sprinkled with salt, and relished like caviar of the earth.

Like the breakfast of one immense, sun-drenched orange in Elche, Spain, quartered, sucked dry, and followed by a handful of dates from palms trees planted by the Phoenicians.

Like the olives savored in a café in Jaffa, Israel, big as fists, fresh plucked from trees that might have fed Abraham, Jesus, and Mohamed.

Like the glass of red wine, an Amarone, sipped while waiting for a connecting flight at the Marco Polo Airport in Venice, that instantly transformed my extreme fatigue into an inkling of eternity.

Some tastes leap across time, connecting the dots in life's seemingly haphazard trajectory.

Can I ever forget my first boiled lobster lying alien-like on an oval platter, as on a flying saucer, in a seaside restaurant in Guilford, Connecticut, its red antennae beaming the SOS of its demise to the colony still crawling along the ocean bottom, whilst I, an impressionable ten-year-old, simultaneously fearful, lest the pincers bound with red rubber bands snap back to life, and transfixed by the spectacle, attack with nutcracker and spike, crack the carapace, and fork out the sweet meat of its claw?!

That experience was referenced in memory years later when the woman who would become my wife first invited me over to her place. Dressed to kill in a tight-fitting skirt and low-cut blouse with gold sprinkles dusted over her chest, grasping a bottle of bubbly by the neck, she received me at the door, declaring somewhat elusively: "Dinner's in the bathtub." — Where I did indeed find two active crustaceans scuttling about. I dutifully set a great pot of water to boil on the stovetop, popped the bottle, and boiled the beasts — a ceremony we reenact annually on New Year's Eve to mark the moment.

I take my sustenance whence it comes, self-service, short-order or refined, ever grateful to the source. The only precept I adhere to religiously is the ancient law of guest-friendship, by which the host is bound to provide and the guest required to humbly accept the bounty and offer no offense.

So when on a trip with my then wife-to-be to North Africa, the chief of police of El Kelaa des Sraghna, a tiny town in the high central plain of Morocco, into whose home I staggered, sick with sunstroke, on the high holiday of the Äid El Kebir, the day on which the faithful slaughter a ram in remembrance of the bleating beast that Ibrahim sacrificed in place of his son Isḥāq, I peered warily at the small round muscle my host shoved over with his right thumb to my side of the collective silver serving plate.

"Heart?" I asked in all innocence.

Whereupon he matter-of-factly motioned with two fingers between his legs. "Monsieur," he snickered, "there are two!" An honored morsel meant to fortify the fruit of my loins, I had no choice but to chew and swallow, forcing my lips to approximate a satisfied smile.

One humble repast stands out among all others as truly transcendent.

I who am ordinarily repelled by the suffocating fumes of candle wax and frankincense, once sniffed the divine in a church in the former Yugoslavia, where my wife and I honeymooned in '87, oblivious to the imminent winds of war. No suffering cloves of Christ, no sacrosanct essence of martyrdom did I smell, but a fertile scent, an olfactory cornucopia of nature's bounty. It was the Virgin Mary's perfume that made my knees buckle under, me a Jew, constitutionally disinclined to genuflect before the god of the Goyim or his immaculate mother! But I couldn't help myself.

"This must be a place where lovers bow and barren women come to bare their hearts and fill their wombs," I whispered in awe to my wife, herself an atheist skeptic of Catholic culture.

Nostrils twitching with the fragrance of ripeness bursting, I thought I fathomed the mystic meaning of the medieval cult of the Virgin (a cult rekindled a few years back by new sightings in a village nearby) when all of a sudden, the flimsy bundles I was clasping disintegrated in my hands, East Bloc brown wrapping paper being a poor prophylactic for the ooze of fruit.

The source of my epiphany, as it turned out, was not the incense burning in some slow swinging censer, but the overripe plums and tomatoes we'd bought at the open-air market just outside the church, unintentionally crushed and vaporized by my sweaty grip.

And when later we picnicked in the woods nearby on what was left, along with some dry bread, I couldn't resist the effect of the red flesh and sweet nectar, nature's aphrodisiac. Our firstborn was the fruit of that culinary revelation.

Wurst Lust

"Alles hat ein Ende, nur die Wurst hat zwei."
(Everything comes to an end, only the sausage comes to two.)

—German Saying

What is it, I wonder, about the German fondness for the flesh of the pig and the Jewish abhorrence of it? Like lust, revulsion too is a visceral thing fueled by the same hunger, only in reverse, a passion linked to the salivary glands that passes down the gullet to tantalize and taunt the gut. For German-speaking Jewish refugees, like my parents, it was a constant tug of war. My mother would not permit it in our home, but my father had to have his weekly fix.

They and others like them came to a culinary compromise at Bloch and Falk, a short-lived kosher idyll of Wurst founded by Berlin émigrés that briefly thrived and then sadly disappeared, as a consequence of changing demographics, on 37th Avenue, near the corner of 74th Street, in Jackson Heights, Queens, today's Little Bombay where now Indians, Pakistanis, and Sikhs vie with their conflicting tastes and taboos.

In that Jewish replica of German Wurst-lust, the reprehensible pig-craving was painstakingly and precisely transposed, or rather reformed, into a kosher cow-craving. But even as a boy, I fathomed that, to get the flavors right, or at least to find a fair Kosher approximation for pork sausage, some enterprising Jewish butcher armed with a meat grinder and a willing tongue, had at least temporarily to suspend his Semitic aversion and embrace Teutonic taste whole-hog, so to speak, applying a Talmudic rigor to isolate and translate porcine products, and beef them up for a Jewish palate.

How well do I remember the grand opening, with banners unfurled and mountains of open *Brötchen* (sandwiches) stacked tall, free for the picking, stuffed with slabs of sausage and smoked meat of every description, Teewurst, Krakauer, Kopfkäse, Jägerwurst, Leberwurst.

From near and far they came, the strongly like-accented refugees of my parents' generation, *Refugln*, as we lovingly called them — which to my childish ear, sounded a lot like *Geflügel*, poultry — they had, after all, flown the coop, dressed to a T in tie and jacket or skirted suits, German from head to toe, save a few recalcitrant curls and the sadness of traumatic loss that never quite muffled their innate exuberance. Waiting patiently on line, with their little native-born progeny in tow, their mouths watered for a licensed taste of the Old Country.

One woman, I recall, got so excited approaching the counter she could not control herself and succumbed to a nervous cough that sounded suspiciously like a dog's bark.

"*Bitte, Lise!* Please control yourself!" her mortified husband looked aghast.

But she couldn't help it, and in any case, nobody but me seemed to notice, each customer consumed by his or her own craving. Was it an involuntary response to the scent of sausage, I wonder, or just a bad case of the hiccups mythologized in memory?

But on Saturdays, when Bloch and Falk was closed, and my father, a man of prodigious appetite, wanted a taste of the real thing, my understanding mother turned a blind eye, and let him take my brother and myself along to Schaller und Weber, the German deli in Manhattan, a kind of culinary brothel in my book, to sample a thick slab of forbidden flesh cut off a fresh hot loaf of *Leberkäse*, still steaming under the knife. Sliced by a bald-headed counterman with gold-capped teeth and a grin straight out of a Georg Grosz drawing, it was the incarnation of what he'd fled. I watched my father savor every bite.

Adventures in the French Digestive Tract

The cliché is that the French are obsessed with sex. But I would argue that if the French, and Parisians in particular, are fixated on anything, it is, rather, their digestion. Farfetched as it may, at first, appear, Paris being densely populated and most Parisian habitats consequently being as compact and tightly packed together as the inner organs, stairways and elevators metaphorically recapitulate the function of the organism, stirring in the ascent, digestive in the descent. It has always seemed to me as if those narrow flights of winding steps and minuscule elevators the size of shopping baskets dangling by a cord that you find in the French capital had something intestine-like about them. As if they had been modeled after the human body, powered by the same dynamic of peristaltic motion. This at any rate is my interpretation based on the ascent and descent of many a winding flight of steps and snug lift, and the consumption of countless meals over the 30-plus years of intimate nibbling with my wife, Claudie, a French native.

New Yorkers suffer heartburn. Parisians complain of *"crise de foie"* (liver crisis). The great gastronome Jean Anthelme Brillat-Savarin, author of *The Physiology of Taste*, the serious eater's bible, summed up the French attitude to food: "Those persons who suffer from indigestion, or who become drunk, are utterly ignorant of the true principles of eating and drinking."

The French meal from beginning to end might well be conceived as a ritualized teasing of the intestines: from the opening *"amuse geule"* (throat tickler) or *"amuse bouche"* (mouth amusement), those unexpected tidbits intended to stimulate the taste buds and arouse the enzymes, along with the accompanying aperitif drink, to the coffee and digestif at dinner's end, everything is geared to facilitating smooth waves of peristalsis as the key to happiness.

*

Cities have certain distinctive sounds. I identify my native New York, for instance, with the honk of car horns periodically punctuated, particularly at night, by the whine of police and ambulance sirens that penetrate the soundest sleep. As if the city were in a perennial rush and you ran the risk of being run over even in your dreams.

The sound I most closely associate with Paris is the resonant clatter of cutlery against plate and the accompanying clink of glasses. This distinctive tinkle reverberates from open windows, outdoor café terraces and restaurants three times a day, at breakfast-, lunch- and dinnertime, calling the faithful to table, as in former times the toll of the church bell called to mass. The French meal remains a sacrament of sorts — This is my body! This is my blood! —bread and wine still being the symbolic bonding agents. French children are taught early, simultaneous with their toilet training, how properly to wield knife and fork and to sit still at the table. Adolescents often engage in more raucous consumption, deliberately muddling the domestic melody and adding a cacophonous clang to anger their elders, but they know the rules and will mellow out and harmonize with age.

It is an exquisite pleasure to listen to the table music of Paris: from the piccolo tinkle of the appetizer dish, to the deep bass clink of cutlery against dinner plate, a passionate polka of knife and fork, to the soprano serenade of dessert fork against dessert plate, the whole interspersed with sotto voce gossip, perfectly timed trills of laughter, and the cymbal clash of wine glasses colliding in a toast, followed by the closing notes of plunked sugar cube, spoon striking cup, and the tinkle of the small change in the tip dish by way of applause.

*

It all begins at the boulangerie. Whereas the béret, the once prototypical headgear of the French, has, except for a few shepherds in the Pyrenees, largely faded from view, the baguette, that proud symbol of the Gallic palate, remains omnipresent. Twice a day, in the morning and again at noon, rain or shine, you can see armies of men, women, and children marching home with a long loaf in hand.

Behold, two men walking, one gripping a baguette, punctuating his observations with a furtive nibble broken off the end. The gist of their exchange may well be of limited interest, but the actions relating to the baguette, a cross between an edible baton and an abbreviated walking stick, are telling. Whereas the American would rather hide his bread in a paper bag, the French cherish the object itself as much as its nutritive value. Not to touch the golden brown crust of the bread of which you are about to partake is as inconceivable to a Parisian as not to catch a preliminary glimpse of the fish you are about to eat, eyes popping out of its head, or not to tenderly caress the partner with whom you are about to make love.

*

Believing as I do that the incidentals, in life as in a meal, matter at least as much and perhaps more than the main dish, permit me to digress concerning the lowly and often neglected pickle.

In the past, I had always been an enthusiastic, indeed a fanatical proponent of the sour, garlic, pickled cucumber, a large, bold, firm, warty green finger of taste, hardly noticing that curled pinky of a pickle, the dainty little French cornichon, but I have recently come to reconsider. Assuming on my last extended stay in Paris that the large (700 gram) jar of Maille cornichons, designated as "Grand Croquant" (or Big Crunch) according to the label, would last us for at least a month or two worth of lunches and midday snacks, I was astounded to discover its contents rapidly dwindling, with no other likely culprits than my wife and myself.

Dating back to 1747, the label proclaims that Maille cornichons are the product "of a rigorous selection process [...] prepared according to a unique recipe, blending vinegar and *pointes d'estragon* (tarragon tips), to bring you," the company promises, "freshness and crunch."

I have long debated the relative virtues of various gherkins with my son, Jacques, a lean and hungry young man, who has been known to go through an entire jar of cornichons in a single sitting. "It's the crunch factor," according to Jacques, that and the sharp vinegary brine, as well as the dainty size, that make the cornichon so enticing.

A sour Polish pickle remains a serious commitment, akin to a Cuban cigar, whereas the furtive snacker with "*un petit creux*" (literally a little hollow in the stomach), can dally in a non-committal fashion with the coquettish cornichon, popping one after another in the mouth without spoiling his appetite. The plastic inner pickle-lifting mechanism inside the jar, a kind of pickle elevator, makes nibbling easy, amusing and un-messy. There is the aesthetic factor too. The little green fingers are interspersed with tiny, white, pickled, dwarfed onions, the spectacle of which on view through the glass wall of the jar reminds of the tiny trinkets we pined after as children, mingled among the round, hard, colored penny gum balls in the luncheonette dispenser.

Before you know it, the jar is empty, consumed by the furtive pickle fairies that lurk in the kitchen and only come out when you're not looking.

*

Then there's mustard, the French dressing of choice. The great French-Jewish 11th-century theologian Shlomo Yitzchaki (aka Rashi), a native of Troyes, in Champagne, who combined biblical scholarship with the wine business, wrote in one of his little known commentaries that the patriarch Abraham dished out calves tongue dipped in mustard to serve to the angels who called on him. Whether true or apocryphal, this tantalizing Talmudic tidbit attests to a longstanding French fondness for the spicy condiment prepared from crushed mustard seed.

Already cherished by the Romans, mustard seed and the recipe for preparing the paste was exported to the outlying Roman colonies in Gaul. This was later picked up and refined by enterprising monks with plenty of time on their hands in between matins and vespers, the same folks responsible, incidentally, for the metamorphosis of fermented grape juice into vintage wine, the brewing of hops and malt into beer, and the distillation of such divine spirits as Benedictine and Chartreuse. Spartan as their diet was, perhaps because they consumed so little and every bite mattered, the monks knew a thing or two about taste.

By the 13th century, Dijon, the capital of the prosperous and powerful Duchy of Bourgogne, became the mustard-making capital of the world. Accorded an Appellation d'origine controlée (AOC) in 1937, subsequently revoked, Dijon mustard still comes incontestably close to the Platonic ideal of mustard.

The ancient Greeks used it to ease the sting of the scorpion. American baseball pitchers allegedly still wipe it on their round projectile as the secret of an un-returnable fast ball. In India the seed is spread around the house to ward off evil spirits. In Germany new brides are said to surreptitiously sew it into the hems of their gowns to assert covert control of the household.

But far more than a mere condiment, unguent or magic charm, in France, bona fide *Moutarde de Dijon*, prepared as per law from black mustard seed (brassica nigra), wine vinegar, salt and citric acid, is a catalyst — though I don't pretend to understand the chemistry, precisely what happens when you blend the enzyme myrosinase found in mustard seed with glucosinolates and water, the colder the water the hotter the mix — that binds with the flavor of certain bland white meats, like chicken, turkey and rabbit, performing veritable alchemical wonders in the roasting pot, fricassee, or frying pan.

One cannot help but wonder if *Moutarde de Dijon* may not have been the key ingredient in the magic elixir sipped for fortitude by the cartoon character Asterix, the French equivalent of Popeye's spinach.

*

But now, on to the true French nitty-gritty. A dazzling display of every conceivable kind and cut of meat, whole, chopped, ground, and squeezed into sausage sheaths, along with prepared charcuterie, sliced *tête de veau* (veal's head), *salade de museau* (muzzle salad), *choucroute*, assorted *pâtés*, and poultry, large and small, lying head to tail, the whole lot straight out of an 18th-century still life, beckon from the refrigerated glass display case under the counter. I feel a bit like a cultivated beast of prey, my mouth watering, gullet twitching, and stomach growling at the killed and chilled array of carcasses before me, the thrill of the hunt sublimated into a civilized exchange of flesh for cash, every time I visit a French butcher.

The Boucherie de la Rue de Bretagne, my purveyor of choice for the six months I lived in the Marais, in the Third Arrondissement, features such a varied selection of steaks and chops, pre-rolled oven-ready roasts, and festooned fowl, I always allowed myself the leisure to salivate, getting dizzy-eyed, before choosing.

On one memorable occasion I opted for quail. The butcher on duty, a genial, portly gent with a sleepy gaze and a bushy mustache like a brace of feathers or a misplaced lion's mane on his upper lip, had just finished surgically removing the veins from a cut of liver for a previous customer, and proceeded to burn off residual feather stubs on my birds with a blow torch, and patiently string them up with strips of bacon.

Meanwhile, *la patronne* (the proprietress) held forth from her perch at the cash register, cheerfully clucking her recipe. "First dice and sauté an onion and a carrot or two in a cocotte, my dear, with a dab of butter to keep your oil from burning," she advised, "then brown the birds on both sides, douse with a cup and a half of dry white wine, and simmer for forty minutes or so, and shortly before serving, add a dribble of cream to bind and thicken the sauce!" She made light of accepting my money with a faintly flirtatious wink: "When's dinner?"

While the fabled green cast iron arches of Les Halles, Paris' erstwhile central market, dubbed by novelist Émile Zola "the Belly of Paris," have gone the way of all flesh, every French boucherie worthy of the name still treats the carving of meat as a sacred ritual, with pagan roots dating back to the Roman Cult of Mithras, to which I remain a willing witness.

*

Next stop the brasserie, the altar of the French appetite!

We are a few years late for the centennial celebration of the founding in 1913 of the classic Brasserie Le Zayer, the same year Stravinsky premiered his ballet *The Rite of Spring* in Paris and the wheels of the Tour de France first whizzed around the French hexagon, and a year before Europe hurled itself into the collective folly of World War I. But it's always a celebration at Le Zayer, on the Place d'Alésia, in the 14th Arrondissement, the locus of two of my own personal culinary epiphanies.

A red velvet curtain discretely stretched at eye-level across the window permits patrons to peer out, while cloistering the plate from the eavesdropping of passersby on our immaculate consumption. We are seated in an ethereal realm. There is a pristine innocence to the swarm of white linen table cloths gracing the empty tables around us, a bit like a virgin snowfall at dawn before being stomped flat and soiled by the crude heels of the madding crowd.

My own double epiphany took place at table at Le Zayer, and I wasn't even hungry at the time. But my dear friend,

Michael Houseman, an American émigré living in Paris for 40 years and counting, who knows that I am stomach-driven, encouraged me to try the *magret de canard.*

"Duck's too fat," I protested, "and I'm really not that hungry."

"*Magret* is special," he said, cognizant of my carnivorous bent, "it's more like steak. You eat it rare."

The thought of rare poultry repelled me. But the Archangel Michael insisted. "Alright," I demurred, figuring I'd take a polite bite or two.

Can I ever forget that first spectacle of sliced slabs of mallard breast doused with a peppercorn and cream sauce? "This is duck?!" I asked, as if the chef had performed some alchemical wonder, a transubstantiation of poultry into beef. Michael just smiled.

The waiter brought back the menu for dessert.

"Oh, no, I really couldn't!" I protested.

But Michael insisted I try the *tarte tatin.*

Again, I demurred.

How can I describe the first sight and taste of that heavenly confection? It is as if the pastry chef had been standing on his head and tipsy, while caramelizing the apples in butter and sugar, and added the dough as an afterthought to hide his folly. The dish was born of a felicitous accident at the Hotel Tatin, in Lamotte-Beuvron, a little town some 100 miles south of Paris. The story goes that one of the Tatin sisters who ran the hotel absently left the apples she was cooking for a traditional apple pie too long in the pan. Smelling burnt fruit, she tried to fudge it by slapping on a sheath of dough and shoving the pan with the whole mess into the oven. Retrieving the concoction and overturning it onto a plate, she was amazed to discover that, not only did the hotel guests not complain, but they clamored for more. Thus a legendary dish was born.

These two treats, *magret de canard*, duck masquerading as beef, and *tarte tatin*, caramelized apple pie turned topsy-turvy, simple dishes both, comprise for me, the alpha and omega of the edible in my sacred communion with French cuisine.

*

Having already treated you, dear reader, to a proper dessert, let's go light. Homer called it the fruit of the gods. In France it was long considered the fruit of kings. Once a year, Louis XIV is said to have received as a choice homage a single succulent pear along with a case of champagne from the mayor of Rheins, transported by a messenger who declared: "We offer you the best we have, our wines, our pears and our hearts, oh King!"

I always take a slow pleasure, savoring a pear for my lunchtime dessert. Admiring the pert curl of its twig tipped with red wax, I contemplate its perfect shape, that roundness that swells like a falling drop of water narrowing at the nipple, and the thin brown skin that envelopes its white flesh. Only when temptation proves too powerful to resist do I let myself bite in, whereupon my nostrils fill with the fruit's fragrant scent and my mouth drips messily with its sweet nectar like a sloppy infant at the breast or a profligate old roué.

So why are the stems of certain Paris pears dabbed in red sealing wax? I had always assumed it to be a mere decorative flourish, like an earring, or like the waxing of apples in the States to artificially buff their polish. But the proprietor of a fruit and vegetable stand on the Rue Saint Antoine, near Métro Saint Paul, set me straight. "It's to preserve the juice, Sir," he said. The Passe Crassane variety of winter pear is apparently not permitted to ripen on the branch so as to preserve its shelf life. Prolonged storage, up to the six weeks they need to mellow in protected hangers, would ordinarily dry them out, reducing them to the spongy excuses for pears they peddle in New York supermarkets, were it not for the dab of wax that works as a stopper, holding in the precious nectar.

*

My wife's late Uncle Henri, a farmer from the Hautes Alpes, still maintained the legal right, since lost to his heirs, to distill a batch of his pears down to a divine *eau de vie*, of which I have a lone bottle left in our liquor cabinet in New York. It fills me with longing and a certain dread every time I lift the stopper to take a nip, as if the bottle were an hourglass measuring my remaining allotment of pleasure.

More balm than beverage, the *digestif* (spirits) is what a French meal is really all about, a grand finale of gustatory delight that magically kicks off the chemistry of digestion.

All that's left for me now is to wish the reader a hearty: Santé! To your health!

Splendor on the Plate:
A Taste of Rural Piemonte

In Italy's northwest corner, where the Alps relax their grip and the Mediterranean blows salty kisses from beyond the hills, the best of nature and culture meet in the kitchen and marry on the plate.

Take the "*caramelle*," house specialty of the Antica Locanda Piemonte, in Condove, a tiny afterthought of a town wedged in practically at the toenails of the Alps. The décor is spare, the atmosphere subdued. But these teensy, weensy ravioli shaped like candies wrapped in pinched golden dough, with a dollop of chopped prosciutto in the middle and a dribble of basil cream sauce, come close to the Platonic ideal of pasta. Sated, several courses later, I stepped out into the night, the sweet Moscato house grappa sparking my synapses and coursing through my veins. And glancing upward, the ethereal sight of the ruins of the Sacra di San Michele, monastic symbol of Piemonte, glowing golden like a second moon, prompted a wordless prayer: a creamy, doughy, eructated ripple of tastes wrapped 'round a hint of ham that would have made Gloria Vanderbilt wince, but surely made the angels smile.

In the bustling market towns of Roero and Monferrato and the sleepy hilltop hamlets of the Langhe (little tongues of land, in local dialect), the vines bleed wine, the forests ooze wild mushrooms and truffles, and the trees burst into heavenly hazelnuts, all of which find their way to the kitchen.

Truffles are the region's holy grail. Relished by the ancient

Egyptians, the Roman Pliny first waxed eloquent about them in imperial Latin. Winston Churchill and Alfred Hitchcock were among the famous modern connoisseurs.

Dug up in the forest depths in Autumn by specially trained dogs and their notoriously crafty handlers, the *tuber magnatum pico* (prime white truffle) is the nostrum and balm of countless banquets and the secret potion of the Piemontese economy (second only to Fiat cars). There is a Truffle Dog University in Alba, the regional capital of Langhe, at which truffle hunters spend as much as 10,000 Euros to train their sniffing canines. Come mid-September, the Truffle Market in the city's historic center is crowded with stands and ardent devotees. The price can run as high as 500 Euros per hundred grams.

Having come a month too early, I tagged along on a simulated truffle hunt in the nearby hamlet of Torre Bormida. "*Venzi, Pippo!*" the frustrated, and somewhat scruffy, cacciatore egged on his slacking pooch, but the dog was more interested in the ambient scents of passing boars. The inferior black summer truffle I tasted at dinner that night shredded over a plate of *carne cruda* (veal tartare), though quite pleasant as a nutty condiment, hardly filled the nose and rallied the flavors, as I'm told the real thing does. It was August and all I could do was pine.

*

But I got lucky in Bra, the town next door, where the Slow Food Movement, a veritable culinary revolution, first took root.

In 1986, with a group of like-minded friends, Carlo Petrini, a native of Bra, residing in Rome at the time, brandished al-dente penne as edible "weapons" to protest the opening of a McDonald's outlet opposite the Spanish Steps, which Petrini viewed as a desecration. He invited passers-by to join him at a picnic table he'd set up across the street to take it slow. The semi-serious protest subsequently expanded into an international movement aptly dubbed Slow Food, with a snail as its symbol. The movement now comprises over 80,000 members in 104 countries, including the U.S., and espouses a commitment to conviviality and what its founder calls "Eco-Gastronomy," based on a heightened consciousness of the endangered culture of the table.

I was driving around Old Pollenzo, Bra's historic center, in search of l'Agenzia, Slow Food's intellectual and culinary headquarters in the erstwhile palace of the Princes of Savoy. Lost and increasingly hot under the collar, I pulled up before a group of workmen crouching in the shade on their lunch break.

"Which way to l'Agenzia di Pollenzo, please?" I asked in broken Italian.

"Slow down!" a tall, balding, bearded man, who might have been the foreman, replied.

I repeated the question, thinking he'd misunderstood.

"You're already there!" he smiled, nodding at a high metal fence.

Only then did I recognize the face from a magazine profile. Slow Food's founder flashed me a genial smile of welcome. Surprisingly lean for a man committed to the cause of conviviality, his eyes had a prophetic fire, albeit turned down to a slow simmer.

"American!" I bowed my head, as if, in a word, to sum up the problem. Born and bred in the Fifties, the heyday of Fast

Food, fattened on burgers and fries, my palate polluted with artificial food coloring and flavor enhancers, I wanted to fling myself at his feet and beg forgiveness, but he cut me off.

"Chow-di good," he grinned. (Which I, at first, mistook for a Piemontese-inflected greeting or farewell.) "Clam chow-di," he clarified.

"*Ah, sì*," I smiled, an instant convert to the cause, "America's slow soup!"

Carlo kindly directed me to the sprawling palace grounds beyond the gate, where Slow Food runs a hotel, wine bank, renowned restaurant, and the University of Gastronomical Sciences (which opened for classes in 2004), all under one red wrap-around roof. I'd made an appointment to tour the grounds, and was soon drooling over untold liquid holdings in the vault of the Banca del Vino, the unofficial Fort Knox of Italian wines. The Ristorante Guido was closed for Ferragosto, the August break when all of Italy decelerates.

*

Let the speed-freaks wiz by on the autostrada below. In the lush Langhe hills above Alba, you have no choice but to take it slow. The narrow, one-track roads hugging the hillsides and meandering through the vines simply won't tolerate haste.

Among the countless unofficial outposts of Slow Food, Piemonte's plethora of agriturismos, government-accredited farms and wineries, welcome hungry pilgrims.

At the Agriturismo Ca' d' Gal, a winery-turned-inn just outside the market town of Santo Stefano Belbo, I had what the family had for dinner, albeit pleading for *"piccole porzioni"* (small portions). Highlights included bagna càuda, an anchovy and tuna sauce, served over fresh vegetables; tiny homemade ravioli with an herb sauce; roast rabbit in sweet Moscato wine; a Moscato grape ice cream; and a bowl of cugnia, a compote of fruit macerated in — What else? — white Moscato wine. The wines, mostly white, kept coming, followed by a shot or two from the family jug of grappa. I blessed the proximity of my tidy room upstairs and awakened the next morning to the sight of a sea of vines undulating outside my window.

Cesare Pavese, a native of San Stefano Belbo and one of Italy's greatest 20th-century novelists and poets, wrote of this charmed corner of creation:

"Even in the old days we referred to the 'hills' as we might have talked about the sea or the woods...and for me it was not simply a place like any other; it represented an aspect of things, a way of life [...] Behind the tilled fields and the roads, the human dwellings, under one's feet, the age-old, indifferent heart of the earth brooded in the darkness, lived in hollows and among roots, lurked in hidden things [...]"

The same earth sang out at the Agriturismo La Costa in Torre Bormida, set amidst a sentient grove of hazelnut trees, where I spent another night, and relished their exquisite hazelnut cakes for breakfast with my coffee.

The most celebrated of these country inns is the Agriturismo San Bovo perched high in the hills above the town of Cossano Belbo. A family-run wine estate, it was one of the first to open its doors to the public a decade ago. A steady steering hand and a blind eye to the precipice got me there in one piece for lunch.

Weather permitting, lunch is served out on the terrace overlooking the Belbo River Valley, from where you can make out the footpaths of the medieval salt traders and muleteers who carted their goods up from the Mediterranean to the mountains. Savor the serenity but don't be fooled by the remote splendor of the vista! With a shaven head and a savvy twinkle in his eye, Chef-owner Aldo Chiriotti brings a worldly wisdom to his craft. "The traders hauled the salt and spices and brought a demanding palate from beyond the sea," Aldo contends, likewise acknowledging the contribution of the chefs of the Royal House of Savoy, who introduced truffles and a French sophistication.

Among the myriad delights of our allegedly "light" three-hour-long lunch were: stuffed flower of zucchini, lovely and delicate in its violet petal pillow; golden tajarin (the local word for tagliatelle) topped with wild mushrooms; and an herb-baked rabbit with sweet string beans from the garden. A sparkling white Moscato wine would, ordinarily, have kicked off a succession of ever more potent wines with each dish, but I had to call a halt at the light red Dolcetto if I hoped to make it down the serpentine road in one piece.

Back in Cossano Belbo, I stopped in, on Aldo's advice, at the source of his pasta flour, Mulino Marino, one of Italy's last active stone mills, where, in the words of the 82-year old master miller, Felice Marino, "we still honor the flour," grinding seven types of organic grain between a pair of colossal, slow turning millstones. Corn flour infused the air inside the mill with its sweet perfume. "I have known bitterness," Felice, a partisan during World War II, acknowledged, "but life is sweet." And true to his name (which means "happy" in Italian), the old man flashed a smile of profound satisfaction as we stepped outside and broke his home-grown, home-ground, home-baked focaccia together.

*

The vintner, Claudio Alario, in the little town of Diano d'Alba, cracked the same Piemontese smile when we talked wine.

We were seated on barrels in his wine cellar, sampling his aging elixirs, all reds, including a celebrated Dolcetto, a bold Nebbiolo, a "*molto corposo*" (very full-bodied) Barbera, and a downright regal Barolo.

"My father left me a vineyard with one ox and one plough, but that is enough if the ground is good," Claudio affirmed.

"A great wine," I waxed poetic on a Barolo buzz, "is the marriage of heaven and earth."

Claudio's smile took on a skeptical skew. "This is what counts," he said, spitting into his calloused hands. "First comes the work of the ground, then the work of the vine, then the work of the man, and then chance. In the end," he allowed, "it's like a miracle if it all goes right."

Feeling celebratory, Claudio invited me to lunch at the Locanda di Batista, a seemingly simple establishment in town, where we dined on a tasty *carne cruda* (steak tartare) with Parmesan shavings and a porcini mushroom risotto verily exploding with flavor, washed down, of course, by a bottle of his own Barolo.

Born of a felicitous accident in transit, in which a batch of the potent fermented Nebbiolo grape must have lost its sweetness, Barolo, later dubbed "the king of wines and wine of kings," was hand-crafted to compete for body, flavor and longevity with the finest Burgundies. The line of vintners involved in the development of what is arguably Italy's noblest wine included Camillo Benzo, Count of Cavour, the champion of Italian reunification. Cavour's family estate, the Castello di Grinzano Cavour, sits on a hill atop the town of Barolo. In its oldest sector, an 11th-century keep built to defend against the Saracens, the castle houses, among its exhibits and amenities, the Enoteca Regionale Piemontese Cavour, the region's first enoteca, and a museum of wine. Its holdings include Roman amphora and a 1919 bottle of Barolo encased in a pillow of mold and dust. The castle is also, incidentally, the site of an illustrious annual truffle auction, broadcast by closed circuit TV to Las Vegas and other overseas markets.

*

Can there be any more eloquent symbolic reply to the Fast Food banality of McDonald's "golden arches" than the surviving bare stone arches of the First Century Roman aqueduct in Acqui Terme? A spa town since Roman times, hot sulfurous water bubbles forth from the Fontana Bollente in the Medieval quarter.

I soaked in the Stabilimento Regina, a 19th-century bathhouse, in a pool fed by naturally warm spring water, to prime my appetite for lunch. Just down the block from the boiling fountain, on the Via della Bollente, Max and Titti, a genial couple known only by their first names, run Acqui's most renowned eatery, the Ristorante La Curia. There are a reputed 1,500 wines on their wine list and baskets of wild mushrooms of every conceivable color and shape on display as you walk in the door. Most memorable among their signature dishes, in the processional of antipasti that precede a proper Piemontese meal, are *filetto baciato* (literally "kissed" filet) of pork wrapped in aged salami from the nearby village of Ponzone, and *tonno di coniglio*, rolled rabbit with poached pear, followed by a plate of *capretto*, baby goat, with a mushroom mousse flan.

Culinary revelation struck again at dinnertime at the Hotel Acqui, located on the Corso del Bagno, the town's lively night-time promenade, where I was comfortably lodged. Gianna dei Bernardi, the tall and regal proprietress and high priestess of the hearth, summed up Piemonte's culinary credo, while overseeing service: "In my cuisine, we don't have big-name chefs, but we have our passion for simplicity. Every dish must sing. With your tongue, you hear the beat of my heart!"

"Simplicity," Gianna maintains, "is the secret of Piemontese cooking. Ingredients are not so much mixed as introduced to each other." Her tender filet of *vitelloni* is a succulent case in point. An Italian classification of meat from Piemonte's own breed of Fassone cattle raised to a maximum of 18 months, just beyond veal and not yet beef, *vitelloni* is fed only on milk and bread. Briefly seared in olive oil before landing on the plate — forgive the candy cliché — the meat literally melts in your mouth. But perhaps the most surprising part of the meal was the *mostarda d'uva*, a kind of Piemontese chutney comprising macerated fruit, served side by side with *robiola di Roccaverano*, a local goat cheese. And just when I was about to cry Uncle, Gianna dished out her trademark *torrone canelin*, a soft, creamy frozen parfait made of hazelnut and whipped egg white, washed down with a sweet red aromatic sparkling Bracchetto d'Acqui.

*

Once a pilgrim's stop on the road to Rome, the ancient town of Gavi — allegedly the birthplace of Ravioli — is guarded by a foreboding fortress carved into the rock of a strategic promontory. Genoese traders built their country villas in the surrounding hills, attracted by the serenity and the fragrant wine, mostly of the white Cortese grape. Today the fortress doubles as a museum and a center for the study of phylloxera, the parasite that once destroyed the fruit of Europe's vines.

Gavi wines can be most pleasurably sampled at an afternoon tasting at the Villa Sparina, a family-owned 17th-century winery in nearby Monterotondo. Salamis and hams hang from the ceilings of the wine cellar, aging along with the wine. Upstairs in the tasting room, on the enological counsel of co-owner Stefano Mocagata, a merry man of great girth, I alternated sips of his estate-grown Villa Sparina Brut (a delightful dry bubbly), his fine-nosed Gavi di Gavi, and his peppery aged Monterotondo Black Label, all gifts of the Cortese grape, with smoky snippets of *lardo, copa,* and *panchetta.* The estate includes the lavish L'Ostellerie, a high-style luxury hotel, at which I lodged, surrounded by 100 hectares of rolling vineyards and forests.

I dined in town that night at the Cantine del Gavi, a restaurant housed in a 16th-century structure, famously run for three decades and counting by chef-owner Alberto Rocchi. A solemn, bespectacled man, he served up a medley of masterpieces from his kitchen in an almost cerebral silence. These included his savory signature *Risotto al Gavi,* steeped in cheese and white Gavi wine; *ravioli al tocco,* stuffed with chopped vegetables and doused with a hot wine sauce; and a tender filet of pork topped with Porcini mushrooms. (Some of Italy's finest wild *funghi* are said to grow in Gavi.) Following a privileged peak at his 14th-century vaulted wine cellar, on Chef Rocchi's recommendation, I concluded the meal with a tongue-tingling grappa from the Distilleria Gualco, in Silvana Dorba, distilled of red wine grapes and 18 different herbs.

The chef toasted me with an old Piemontese saying: "*Chi va piano va sano e va lontano.*" (He who moves slowly, stays healthy and lives long.)

*

I know I'll never taste another ravioli like the "*caramelle*" in Condove. Still, Piemonte is a kind of edible Eden, a paradise not quite lost with portable implications for life in the fast lane. Farmers Markets are catching on, I've noticed, in big cities across America. People are reclaiming their palates. It's a start. Maybe it's time to send Old McDonald back to the farm where he belongs.

The Golden Valley of Ale

For nine centuries, the faithful have wended their way through the deep dark forest of Merlanvaux to the Cistercian Trappist Abbey of Notre-Dame d'Orval, nestled in the bucolic splendor of the Val d'or (Golden Valley), in Belgium's Ardennes Mountains. Nowadays they mostly come for the beer. The light amber-hewed ale brewed on its premises, according to venerable recipe and strict quality control, is pure liquid prayer.

One of six brews graced with the Trappist label (five of which are produced in Belgium), they collectively constitute the gold standard in beer.

Orval and its brother beers (Chimay, Rochefort, Westmalle, and Westvleteren) can indeed be sampled elsewhere, at countless Belgian tavern tables and well-stocked supermarket shelves, and are exported to select outlets abroad. But a visit to the Abbey of Notre-Dame d'Orval with its sprawling ancient ruins hallows the flavor. The mighty fir trees of the surrounding forest bow their green heads and the old stones whisper, putting you in just the right frame of mind to appreciate the complex mingling of bitter and sweet that makes a great beer. For here, at the southwest rim of the Ardennes Mountains (seemingly far away from it all, though actually only a two-and-a-half-hour drive from Brussels), you can quench your thirst at the source.

The Mesopotamians first sucked on dampened sops of moldy bread to get a buzz. Egyptians likewise indulged. But it was the Celts who developed a real predilection for the blend of water, malt, sugar, and hops, and generations of medieval monks who refined its fermentation into a sacred art. According to the British beer authority, Michael Jackson (not to be confused with the late American pop singer of the same name), Belgium is the true birthplace and home of the blessed beverage of the Celts.

They sip it and savor it, before, after, and during meals; stew and simmer all sort of poultry, meat, and fish in it; smother succulent North Sea mussels in its frothy broth; and even cure what ails them with a draught. According to local legend, St. Arnoldus, the patron saint of brewers, who lived at the height of the Plague years, plunged his staff into a vat of beer and all who drank of its contents were cured. (Needless to say, Belgian brewers keep his statue close to their vats.) Beer is also said to be especially good for breast-feeding, as it stimulates the lacteal glands.

Tell that to the Trappists, whose order, derived from the Cistercian tradition established by St. Bernard of Clair-vaux, is among the most austere contemporary remnants of medieval religious life. The active sector of the Orval Abbey (where some 40 monks still adhere to the vows of silence and a strict regimen of work and prayer) is off-limits to visitors. True to Cistercian custom, the monks must earn their keep. Consequently, outsiders may enjoy the fruits of their labors, including Trappist whole-wheat bread and Port Salut-style cheese sold at a gift shop. The brewery is managed by a private concern.

The abbey, which celebrated its 900th anniversary in 1970, has gone through numerous architectural and spiritual incar-nations since its original founding by itinerant Benedictine monks from Calabria, Italy. The Benedictines departed, and a small community of Canons took over, who subsequently affiliated themselves with the Cistercians, who, in turn, fell under the sway of the rigid strictures of the Abbey of La Trappe. Then, in 1793, a French revolutionary army ravaged the abbey and forced the brotherhood to disband. Today's monumental structure, rebuilt by the architect Henry Vaes on the same site and inspired by medieval designs, was completed in 1948. Vaes also designed the distinctive chalice-like glass in which the beer is served.

The visitor can build up a mighty thirst wandering through the ruins. They include a modernized 13th-century *maison d'accueil*, formerly used to welcome noble guests, now the site of an audiovisual installation on Trappist life; the remains of a 12th-century cloister and a haunting 16th-century portal silhouetted against the sky, all hewn in the ocher-colored — one might well say "beer-colored" — rock of the region. The rose window in the north arm of the transept, the Romanesque capitals, and Gothic pillars are all that's left of the medieval church. A medicinal herb garden recalls the monks' role as healers.

The circular Fountain of Mathilda is the source of the spring water still used for the beer. It is said that the Countess Matilda, Duchess of Tuscany, widow of Godfrey the Hunchbacked, leaned over the well's edge in 1076 and accidentally dropped her wedding ring in, and that a trout retrieved it for her, whereupon she was moved to exclaim: "Verily, this is a 'val d'or,' a golden valley!" Thus, by the inversion of popular parlance, the name Orval and the image on the bottle label of a fish rearing upright biting on a golden ring. However farfetched, the legend adds a fittingly marvelous dimension to the beer.

If the bubbly brew looks alive as you pour it into your glass, well, it is. Additional yeast is added during the bottling process. Re-fermented Trappist ales are among the only beers that age in the bottle. The adept un-cap the bottle gently and pour it just right, tilting, not topping the bottle, leaving behind a yeasty residue (to be swallowed separately for its vitamin B content). The richness and relatively high alcohol content of Trappist brews (Orval 6.2 percent and Westvleteren, the strongest, 11.5 percent) definitely make them "*bières de dégustations*," beers to be sipped and savored, not gulped or chugged. While the other four tend to be ambrosial (Westvleteren, an almost chocolaty beer, Westmalle, Chimay, and Rochefort only a bit less unctuous), Orval is the driest beer of the lot, and the only one you'd really want to drink along with your meal.

For those so inclined, just outside the gates of the monastery, the *Auberge l'ange gardien* (Inn of the Guardian Angel) serves up a heaping plate of thick-sliced Ardennes ham, another culinary treasure of the region, along with the abbey's bread, to be washed down naturally by a glass of Orval.

Beer is Belgium's lifeblood, the source and symbol of its unique vitality. Among the several hundred quality Belgian brewers, large and small, Orval and its fellow Trappists unquestionably set the standard. "Liquid bread" to the monks who once depended on its nutritional value to supplement a spare diet, today it's liquid gold to thirsty connoisseurs around the world.

Still Brewing Strong: Café Culture in Vienna

The word café is French, the drink itself of Turkish extraction, but the classic Occidental *locus bibendi*, that civilized refuge from civilization, was born and bred in Vienna. Menaced by the ever-accelerating pace of modern life, reports of its imminent demise notwithstanding, the coffeehouse is alive and well in Austria's capital city. Here at last count, in any one of Vienna's 300 plus cafés worthy of the name, in surroundings cozy or sprawling, simple or lavish, humming or hushed, you can still put your cares on hold, nurse a single cup through a long afternoon, nibble on a strudel, or succumb to the lure of pastries fit for an imperial palate. The vintage establishments featured below are representative of the best. A traveler with time and inclination to wander the winding streets of the old city and outlying districts will discover many others.

But first, a little history to stir the appetite. In true Viennese fashion, the origins of the institution are rooted in legend and intrigue. Two 17th-century spies, Georg Franz Kolschitzky and Johannes Diodato, share claim to the title of first purveyor of coffee. Both were undercover agents during the second Turkish siege of Vienna in 1683, gathering military intelligence behind enemy lines for Austrian Emperor Leopold I. It had long been held that Kolschitzky happened upon a stash of coffee beans left by the Turks, mistaken by others for animal feed. And since his information proved reliable and ultimately contributed to an Austrian victory, the Emperor allegedly granted his erstwhile spy the right to sell the enemy's elixir. And so, the legend goes, Kolschitzky (who had a street named after him) opened Vienna's first coffeehouse, Zur blauen Flasche (At the Blue Bottle) and the Viennese have been sipping happily ever after. A revisionist historian, however, rattled the legend, unearthing a bona fide imperial license, dated 1685, which gave Diodato, not Kolschitzky, the right to sell coffee at another site. Whichever version is true, the coffeehouse was born and others followed.

Exclusively devoted at first to dispensing coffee, these primitive locales soon added tiled stoves to lure customers in out of the cold, card and billiard tables and newspaper racks as incentives to linger. The coffeehouse craze swept Vienna and spread in the 18th century throughout Europe, becoming particularly popular in Paris. Further refined in the 19th century, the café reached its heyday at the Fin de Siècle and later crossed the Atlantic.

In Vienna, this paradoxical locus of relaxed intensity fueled by caffeine, coddled by plush cushions, sweetened by fancy cakes, proved fertile ground. Here dreams were first coaxed into the analytic light of day, modernity was imagined and designed, and the world order was altered like the pieces on a chessboard.

Every Viennese café worth its beans cultivates its reputation. The Café Griensteidl, near the Hofburg, was the favorite haunt of literati like Arthur Schnitzler, playwright of such racy fare as La Ronde; Felix Salten, creator of the children's classic, Bambi (as well as, rumor has it, the anonymous "adults only" classic, Josephine Mutzenbacher); and another journalist and sometime dramaturg, Theodor Herzl, who later went into the nation-building business. Another legendary haunt, The Café Central, long defunct, reopened at its original location,

Herrengasse 14, in 1983. Home to the original "bohemian" poet Peter Altenberg, it also served as headquarters to Russian revolutionaries Lev Bronstein (aka Leon Trotsky) and his calculating chess partner Vladimir Ilyich Lenin.

For a whiff of the real thing, contemporary purists flock to the Café Hawelka, the most austere and compact of the great cafés. Nestled on the narrow Dorotheergasse, just off the Graben, a hop, skip and a jump, or as the Viennese would say, "*ein Katzensprung,*" (literally a cat's leap) from St. Stephen's Cathedral. Heaven forbid you ask the prickly little waiter for an ordinary cup of coffee. "There is no ordinary coffee here!" he has been known to enlighten the uninformed. Aficionados order a Mélange, a large cup of coffee with a froth of hot milk and a dash of whipped cream. As per ritual, your coffee is served on a tiny metal tray with a jar of sugar cubes and a glass of water. The sign outside welcomes "*Künstler und Lebenskünstler*" (artists and artists of life), a throwback to the Post-War period, when regulars included painter Ernst Fuchs, novelists Heimito von Doderer and Nobel laureate Elias Canetti, and conversations could get as intense as the coffee. Newspapers scattered about or strung on bamboo poles make most of the reading matter nowadays.

The current proprietor, Günther Hawelka, a tall, kindly, doe-eyed man, works the counter and personally, lovingly, brews the coffee. "The Hawelka is a living legend!" he smiles, guarding a sacred trust passed on from his 87-year-old dad, who still drops by for his daily cup. Don't expect much in the way of nibbles. A piece of plum cake and a ham sandwich is all you'll get. But the atmosphere is as authentic as the coffee and the waiter's acerbic lip.

For a light snack, or what the Viennese call *Jause,* repair to Trzesniewski's across the street. For close to a century and counting, this cramped little standing-room only buffet bar has been dishing out a savory array of "*belegte Brötchen*" (open-faced finger sandwiches) of chopped chicken liver, herring and the like, washed down by a Lilliputian Pfiff (a 1/8th liter glass) of draft beer. At a pittance a pop, your purse and stomach can afford an assortment.

Undoubtedly Vienna's most lavish and illustrious café is the K. u. K. Hofzuckerbäcker Ch. Demel's Söhne (His Majesty's and Imperial Highness' Royal Confectioner Christoph Demel's Sons), Demel's for short. Located on the Kohlmarkt, an elegant, pedestrians-only shopping street at the far end of the Graben, the fabled confectioner has changed hands and site since its founding in 1786. Dense with chandeliers and ornate murals of frolicking water nymphs, the baroque decor can get a bit unctuous. In high summer season, swarming with tourists, Demel's sometimes seems like a "Disney" remake of itself. And the dour waitresses in their stern black habits could well be mistaken for an order of austere nuns devoted to disciplining naughty hedonists. But the dazzling spectacle of glass cabinets teaming with chocolate, trays heaped with cookies and biscuits, and tier upon tier of pastries of every conceivable shape, color ,and contents, makes Demel's a shrine to sweet-toothed devotees. With a trembling finger you point out your selection, take a number, and faint with craving, bide your time over coffee while waiting to be served.

The dictionary defines *Torte* as "fancy cake," but, in truth, there is no apt English equivalent. For the Viennese *Torte* is to any other cake as turtle-dove to pigeon or diamond to coal. Demel's *Gerollte Mandeltorte* (multiple rolled layers of ganache, meringue, almond and buttercream), the *Nusscafétorte* (a nut and coffee cream cake), the Nelson, Senegal, and mocha cream, to mention only a few offerings, make a pilgrimage a must. But be prepared to wait for a table.

Back on the Graben, epicures in a hurry can find a tantalizing assortment of goodies-to-go at Julius Meinl, the original and sole surviving Viennese-owned outlet of a chain of gourmet markets founded in 1826, more recently sold to a foreign investor. The proximity of the Pestsäule, the gaudy monument to victims of The Plague, paradoxically underlines the local commitment to worldly delights.

A brisk walk back along the Kohlmarkt, through the yard of the Hofburg (the imperial palace), across the majestic Heldenplatz (Heroes' Square), and along the immaculate lawns and flower beds of the Volksgarten (People's Park) will let you out on a busy corner of the Ringstrasse. This monumental thoroughfare modeled on Paris' Champs Elysées literally rings around the old city, following the foundations of the medieval wall. Traffic can get tangled, with streetcars, automobiles, and Fiakers (horse drawn carriages) jockeying for right of way. All the more reason to seek asylum in the sumptuous Café Landtmann right there on the Ring, next door to the Burgtheater (Imperial Theater).

Catering to a lively mix of theatergoers and players, politicians from the Rathaus (City Hall) and Parliament just across the Ring, journalists and foreign correspondents, professors from the nearby University, and anybody else, this café (the back room of which once housed the royal stables) epitomizes in its understated elegance the Viennese ideal of "*Gemütlichkeit*," or congeniality. Celebrating its 125th anniversary in 1998, the place has played host to the likes of the Duke of Windsor, Julian, Queen of the Netherlands, Thomas Mann,

Gary Cooper and Marlene Dietrich, among other celebrities who signed the guest book, and Sigmund Freud, who took his regular morning coffee here. Hardly content, however, to sit on its laurels, The Landtmann eschews a high gloss profile, maintaining a subtle balance of refinement and relaxed informality. The inlaid mahogany walls, burgundy plush cushions and impeccable black tuxedos of the waiters — all to be hailed as "*Herr Ober!*" (headwaiter) — confirm the pedigree. And true to tradition, whatever your tab and however long you linger, the waiter will not trouble you with a bill until you strenuously flag him down.

The Landtmann offers complete meals or snacks, as a prelude to further indulgence. A bowl of *Rindsuppe mit Fleischstrudel* (a savory beef bouillon with a floating slice of paté baked in filo dough) makes a light meal unto itself. In addition to the 19 available varieties of coffee (including a Mazagran iced with a dash of rum, an Einspänner with a dollop of cream in a tall glass, a Türkischer poured piping hot from a long-necked copper pot and, of course, the classic Mélange), you will not be scolded for ordering a "decaf." Kids can pick from six styles of hot chocolate. Standards in The Landtmann's luscious line of *Mehlspeisen* (pastries) are the *Mozarttorte*, a harmony of pistachio and truffle cream over a thin chocolate biscuit; the *Husarentorte*, a hazelnut and caramel cream standing guard over a walnut base; and the *Marillentorte*, an apricot mousse covered with whipped cream topped by apricot slices and green leaves of marzipan. Sugarless cakes for diabetics are also available on request.

For a modernist alternative, The Café Prückel, elsewhere on the Ring, reflects the innovative aesthetic of The Wiener Werkstätte, the famous school of design, whose work is featured across the street at the MAK (Museum of Applied

Arts). The ceilings are high, the seating comfortable and the crowd eclectic.

It would be heresy to overlook the Café im Hotel Sacher, beside the Wiener Staatsoper (the Opera). Here in opulent splendor, an oval portrait of the young Empress Elizabeth (Fin-de-Siècle Vienna's Princess Di) gazes down serenely from maroon red walls, bestowing her implied imperial blessing. Though other pastries appear on the menu, the specialty here, the Zen kōan of its kitchen, is unquestionably the famous chocolate cake. Despite the seven egg yolks in the recipe, *Sachertorte* was concocted as an allegedly "light" desert for noble digestion. Its secret is the apricot streak subtly but unmistakably dividing the cake down the middle and underlying its bittersweet varnish of chocolate icing.

Other famous cafés include The Frauenhuber, the city's oldest, where Beethoven sometimes performed; The Mozart, featured in the film noir classic *The Third Man*; The Diglas, noted for its tea and cakes; the post-modern Do & Do Café; and Gustav Mahler's favorite, The Sperl.

Take your pick or, better yet, try them all!

To aid digestion after a binge, you can take a leisurely spin on the Riesenrad, Vienna's famous Ferris wheel, each revolution of which is a full ten minutes long. Or you can repair to the Viennese branch of Weight Watchers centrally located right on the Ring.

IV

Notes of a Native Stranger

Ode to the Great Indoors

A bundle of contradictions, like most, I take pleasure in trips to foreign climes, nuzzling the unknown in limited doses, basking in strangeness, but am invariably relieved to get back home to process the experience. I'm really an indoorsman at heart — as opposed to the outdoorsman of the Teddy Roosevelt ilk. Like Teddy, I, too, get all worked up and winded at times, dreaming of adventure. Unlike him, however, whose manifest destiny it was to puff up his chest and ride rough in the saddle, I prefer to sit soft in my Herman Miller Aeron desk chair, with the moveable lumbar support, shepherding my breath before a window, with the option of either peering out or pulling the shade.

Activity is invigorating, so long as it's not my own. Outdoorsmen hop to it as soon as the thermometer drops, delighting in the chill and challenge of braving the elements. I, on the other hand, am perfectly content to watch the snow fall from within, to the stirring accompaniment of radiator hiss and refrigerator hum.

My wife, a professor of French literature, is similarly inclined. Her favorite work-out room is the library. Once interviewed for a teaching job in Boulder, Colorado, among other questions she was asked: "What do you do in your spare time?" — Translation: What sport do you play? — "Well," she hazarded with feigned enthusiasm, "I could take up bicycling, so long as it isn't too hilly." Fortunately for both of us, she did not get the job.

Not that I'm totally averse to the outside, as I've already

acknowledged. Indeed, I delight in traversing delimited spans.

Take Washington Square Park, for instance, my favorite stomping ground. Having crossed it twice daily, back and forth between home and work, for four and a half decades and counting, the park has metamorphosed in my mind into a kind of terrarium. Ambling past the statue of Signore Garibaldi, hero of Italian unification, stationed to the East, whose dynamic stance notwithstanding, can't quite muster the resolve to draw his sword, I cross at a leisurely diagonal, making occasional eye contact with passersby, drawn by faces beautiful or odd, while dodging the wheelies of adolescent skateboarders, the pitches of drug dealers, and the importunate pleas of panhandlers; I weave my way between the fountain and the victory arch — where, in 1783, George Washington bid farewell to his troops, and in 1917, French conceptual prank-ster Marcel Duchamp and a few artist friends scaled to the summit to proclaim the Independent Republic of Greenwich Village; pausing for a last admiring look at a squirrel scurrying at a sheer vertical up the trunk of the 135-feet-tall, 310-year-old Hangman's Elm, said to be the city's oldest tree, I exit at the park's northwest rim. Invigorated by the crossing of what is technically an outdoors enclave, my spirit encases it, as if within a virtual glass paperweight, the kind that erupts in a snow storm when you shake it and settles when it's still.

As a child, I cherished sick days, when sealed inside my head, I was licensed to stay home and play all day, with the bedroom, otherwise shared with my brother, all to myself. And in Kindergarten, on the days I did attend, at playtime I walled myself in with oversize wooden building blocks, and the teacher had to drag me out, kicking and screaming.

Repelled long after the fact by a pigeon's hot plop, the

dumb bird still cooing victoriously in memory among its kind on the ledge above the entrance to my high school, where somebody always got hit, I prefer my wildlife at a safe remove.

Unlike most, I am even fond of the New York City subway at off-hours, stench and screech notwithstanding, that 245-miles-long tube of track encased in tunnel.

But that's about as much excitement as I can take in one run.

Let others to go sky diving, bungee jumping, and chase butterflies for sport, I am content to make like a caged bird, dreaming of flight.

When the World Came to Queens

In 1964, the world came to my native borough, Queens, which was a good thing, since Queens was going nowhere. A man named Moses prophetically led the multinational minions to the Promised Land, a strip of reclaimed marsh at Flushing Meadow, on the site of a similar mass influx in 1939. But by April of the following year the world went home again, leaving nothing behind but a lot of rubbish and a big rusty globe.

We were on hand to witness the grand finale on April 21, 1965.

Age 12 at the time, I remember standing, greatly stirred at the foot of the "Fabulous Unisphere," the Fair's theme symbol, a globe rising 140 feet above a reflecting pool, with its land masses supported on an open grid of stainless-steel latitudes and longitudes, waiting for something to happen.

"This symbol," my father read aloud from the Official Souvenir Book, "dramatizes the interrelation of the peoples of the world and their hopes for Peace through Understanding. The Fair is dedicated to Man's achievements on a shrinking globe in an expanding universe..."

How, I fretted in silence, can the world be shrinking and expanding at the same time? Picturing the steel rings around the globe as a kind of cosmic rubber band and the globe itself as a shrinking balloon, true child of the Cold War era, I trembled at the seemingly inevitable prospect of the band snapping and the balloon exploding any moment now.

My brother and I were frankly more fixated on the life-sized model of Tyrannosaurus Rex, a mascot for fossil fuels, rearing nearby, teeth bared, claws prone, courtesy of Sinclair Oil.

Later, at General Electric's "Progressland," an electric-powered, walking, talking replica of the American nuclear family, complete with genial, pipe-smoking father, tail-wagging dog, and perennially cheerful children, appeared to function far better than the real thing.

As for Michelangelo's much-touted sculpted marble masterpiece, "The Pietà," on loan at the Vatican Pavilion — what's the big deal, I figured, if it can't even talk or walk!?

I, for my part, was particularly taken by the Coca-Cola pavilion, a microcosm of the world, in every clime of which you can quench your thirst with "the real thing." No woodland trail have I since hiked, but that the natural forest bed failed to live up to that soft green simulated moss carpet with its canned sound effects, courtesy of Coca-Cola, which beverage, as I later learned, is in many places more readily available than dependable drinking water.

Meanwhile, as the World's Fair wound down to its final hour, we made our way to where the Westinghouse Time Capsule was to be lowered into the ground, filled with a Bible, an incandescent light bulb, and some other stuff to be preserved for future generations, hysteria suddenly erupted.

Like the idol worshipers of the Golden Calf in the movie *The Ten Commandments*, people wanted the pay-off now. Up and down the pathways, hooligans went tearing up tulips donated by the Dutch, inspiring ordinary folk to follow suit. Soon every man, woman, and child had a muddy bouquet.

Booty in hand, they surged toward the exits.

Whereupon helicopters took off from the Port Authority Heliport and hovered ominously overhead, like on TV newsreels from Vietnam.

In a panic, people dumped the evidence and tried to wipe suspicious stains from their hands and clothes.

And as the New York World's Fair drew to a close and Mr. Moses ceremoniously presided over the lowering of the Westinghouse Time Capsule into the ground (a testament to the future of Man's aspirations and the prospect of "Peace Through Understanding"), pathways littered with ravaged tulips told a different story[1].

---

[1] Another obsolete symbol of progress, the IBM Selectric typewriter, presented as a sleek futuristic marvel at the Fair, now languishes as a clunky relic, a dinosaur of the information age, on display at the seldom visited Queens Museum, at the site of the long-forgotten Fair grounds.

New York's Unreal Estate

A traveler by definition is a person far from home, and so, receptive to a never-ending stream of impressions aroused by the strange. Might it be possible, I wondered, to alter my perspective, to modify my mindset so as to travel down familiar streets and see them in a new light? It started as a lark, a self-assigned challenge to combat boredom. I sometimes get antsy sitting around between trips, so I decided to reset my reality, or rather my perception of it, to venture out and redis-cover my own city with the eyes, ears, and nose of a deliberate stranger.

I was inspired in this empirical experiment by the story of the discovery of the Paleolithic cave paintings at Altamira, in Santillana del Mar, in northern Spain, which site I was privileged to visit in 1973 before the cave was permanently closed to the public. A local gentleman, Marcelino Sanz de Sautuola, an amateur archeologist, decided to take his young daughter, Maria, along on a Sunday stroll to give her a richer appreciation of her native clime. Maria brought along her little dog. The animal followed its nose, disappearing into the mouth of a cave in which the father had previously discov-ered scattered bones, and the girl trotted in after her pet with a torch. Moments later, the wild-eyed child came running out, crying "Bisons! Bisons!" Signor de Sautuola followed her back in to the spot where the dog stood barking. The man was baffled, seeing nothing but bare rock, until his daughter tilted her head back, by example, and pointed upwards, revealing the magnificent canopy of cave paintings overhead.

Grownups tend, by force of habit, to always view the world from the same angle, while children whose wobbly heads are not yet glued in place still crane their necks to take in the unexpected, wherever it may lodge.

*

Dizzying from close-up, dream-like from afar, New York is a great geometric gorge gouged out of the sky, a towering steel and concrete range teeming with habitation and commerce. It's an evanescent grid of grit and graffiti, the instant collages of torn advertising posters, conversation shreds, the filthy and oftentimes forgotten architectural flourishes of downtown buildings, and the tiny dramas of individuals jostling for dignity and meaning in the mad dash.

A stranger put it succinctly in a random remark I once overheard in passing: "People ask me why I like New York. It's not because it's so great, but because it's going through its Babylonification."

The experiment is ongoing. What follows is a log of selected findings.

Unnecessary Noise Prohibited

"Unnecessary noise prohibited!" commands an enigmatic New York street sign. But what noise is necessary? When hearing a siren whining in the night, I both dread and perversely wish that the emergency be close at hand. To dread it is to send the accident or fire or death as far away as it can go. To wish it adds a morbid luster to a lackluster life, embellishing a private sense of insufficiency. Sometimes I fear that if I listen too hard it will draw the siren to me like a magnet and manufacture a tragedy to match. This is foolish, morbid and infantile thinking, but night makes you infantile, especially when you can't sleep and the darkness itself looks like a bungling indecisive burglar peering in at the window.

Whose Zoo Is It?

Ever since Noah's ark, zoos have brashly asserted humanity's edge as the spectator species perched outside the cage ogling the spectacle species within — a distinction somewhat blurred in New York by the proliferation of window guards and the complex ramifications of the burglar-tenant relationship.

Homo sapiens flock to the zoo to feel superior. But cross-sectioned under Plexiglas, the tireless activity of the ant hill in the Central Park Zoo magnified by a surveillance camera reveals a parallel reality disturbingly similar to our own. Lugging leaves and twigs in lieu of laptops, pocketbooks, and attaché cases, stepping over each other to achieve some unattainable end, these micro-managers in three-piece bodies parody human antics to a tee. Or is it the other way around? Do we make like insects — so assiduous, so driven, so ruthless — commuting to our destiny? Who can deny the striking resemblance between an anthill and a skyscraper?

Invasion of Privacy

Having grown up in a private house, I sometimes experience a sudden terror at the thought of the ceiling caving in and all the others who live on the floors above me literally dropping by.

What's Eating You?

New York apartment houses retain the odors of diverse domesticities; anything roasting, stewing, steaming, or boiling in or on the ovens or the hearts of its inhabitants spills over into the hallway. It is embarrassing to sniff these private smells in passing. You know what your neighbors are eating and what's eating them.

The Olfactory Lure of French Fries

Cleanliness smells pleasantly artificial, filth reeks revoltingly sincere. The odor of fried grease, for instance, is far more intoxicating than the scent of the finest French perfume. Imagine a modern-day Odysseus lashed to the bumper of a bus trying to resist the olfactory lure of French fries.

Urban Bullfighter

Two teenage girls race across a busy intersection, barely eluding a stretch limo. Says one, still giggling, to the other: "At least we'd've been run over in style!" The same madness strikes moody late middle-aged men. One moment I'm a bystander and the next moment I'm a bullfighter, boldly beckoning a bus to my right flank with a broken umbrella as I lean to the left and let it rumble by.

Symphony of Steam

Last winter I spent an entire afternoon listening with silent rapture to the performance of a splendid steam symphony for solo radiator. It was a little like bagpipes, minus the drone, with a hint of snake hiss, pressure cooker sputter, spit dribble, and wordless whisper. Very monotonous, very atonal, I found it strangely soothing, drowning out the racket of chatter emanating from below, a John Cage tour de force accompanied by the Bali shadow puppet play of trees dancing in the wind on the far wall across the courtyard.

Dead Ahead

"You're not looking for that artist fellah, are ya!?" asked a kindly old gentleman with sallow skin and sunken cheeks, seeing me struggling to decipher a rumpled map one Sunday afternoon at the corner of Grape and Sassafras Avenues, at Green-Wood Cemetery, in Brooklyn, the select permanent address of some of the City's late illustrious scattered among the plebs. Watering can in hand, the old man was bent over filling it from a hand pump. "Follow me!" he smiled. "My wife and I are on our way to visit our daughter."

The Misses said nothing, understandably disinclined to share her grief with a stranger, but the old man was naturally gregarious, even in mourning.

"Here we are," — he pointed behind a double row of low-standing tombstones on Lot 44603 that looked like a Lilliputian housing development — "the painter's out back."

Abutting their daughter's plot, the grave of street artist Jean-Michel Basquiat was expressively littered with broken pencil stubs, scribbled notes and doodles, and a wad of wilted paper money from the board game Monopoly held down by a handful of pebbles and small change, among other offerings.

"What a mess!" the old man shook his head. "How much do you figure one of his pictures is worth today?" he wondered aloud, watering the ivy, while his wife silently, disapprovingly, pruned the weeds.

Clearly knowledgeable in local lore, he told me about the time Basquiat, or "that Basket fellah," as he called him, went into a deli in Brooklyn to order cold cuts for a party. "Only the way he looked, you know, with his hair poking out in every direction like a porcupine, the deli owner didn't trust his credit. But he did recognize that other fellah that was with him, must 'a seen him on TV, what's his name, the one with the mop of blond hair."

"Andy Warhol."

"Right. That Warthog fellah had to vouch for him, but in the end, he got his meat. And now, wouldn't ya know," the old man made a mental calculation, "I bet one of his pictures is worth more than the whole delicatessen, cold cuts, pickles, walls 'n all."

Exiting the cemetery near sunset I was serenaded by an eerie twitter. Green-Wood, it turns out, is inhabited by a flock of monk parakeets escaped from a crate that broke open upon delivery at Kennedy Airport sometime back in the Sixties, and have been proliferating, sonorously nesting ever since in the spires of the great brownstone Gothic revival gateway.

Odd Birds

Blocking the path of the Number 2 Uptown Limited bus at the corner of 165th Street and Audubon Avenue, a red-crowned chanticleer escaped from an urban barnyard stood his ground, crowing and refusing to budge.

"Is that really a rooster?!" I asked, incredulous, seated directly behind the driver, with a bird's eye view of the stand-off.

"Well it sure ain't Frank Purdue!" the driver shrugged, impatience competing with a grudging grin of admiration.

*

I spotted the same dogged aviary resolve in the crazed gaze of a red-tailed hawk a thousand miles from its native clime, perched on the topmost branch of a tall tree known as the Hangman's Elm in Washington Square Park. (The Park had once been the site of a gallows.) I'd seen wild turkeys, crows, a cardinal, an owl be born, two sparrows pecking it out to the death, but never a red-tailed hawk. Even the ordinarily unflappable chess players interrupted their game to peer upwards in awe at this incarnation of the inconceivable and unattainable, a mighty king oblivious to the rules of the game who might at any moment pounce on and dispose of some unlucky pawn.

It's Safe as Long as You Feed It

"It's safe as long as you feed it," a man wearing a live python for a necklace reassured a concerned passerby in the park.

What Goes Up Must Come Down

Philippe Petit, the latter-day French Houdini famous for an early morning stroll he took on a high-wire strung between the soaring twin summits of the World Trade Center, was sentenced at the time by an amiable judge with a sense of humor to "perform" community service in the parks.

I saw him walk a slack rope strung between two trees in Washington Square Park. The impish little pug-nosed man with the slender build of a jockey and the eyes and balance of an eagle was warming up, riding a unicycle around the rim of a chalk circle prior to mounting the rope. I will never forget the sudden look of profound displeasure that gripped his beady blue orbs and twisted his thin lips, when, notwithstanding his mimed insistence to stand clear, one hapless spectator had the audacity to toe the line, and worse, to drop a cigarette butt inside the chalked perimeter. Perfectly balanced, the unicyclist stopped dead on an invisible dime, as vexation welled up into disgust. Singed by the laser-like intensity of that disapproving sneer, with all eyes upon him, the owner of the offending toes retracted them forthwith, stooped to retrieve the cigarette butt, and slunk off, whereupon a smiling Petit completed his act.

The second time I saw him, years later, he was walking with a woman I assumed to be his wife, wheeling his offspring, a petit Petit in a pram, a mere mortal making his mundane way along Sixth Avenue, his downcast gaze trying to deflect the woman's displeasure and elude the attention of passersby, apparently in the throes of a domestic spat. How else to explain what happened next?

The fearless funambulist who took his act from the Twin Towers to Sydney Harbour Bridge, the Louisiana Superdome, the concourse of Grand Central Station, and a wire stretched across the Seine from the Palais de Chaillot to the second story of the Eiffel Tower, in each locale carefully calibrating wind shifts and weather conditions, had somehow miscalculated one of those buckled welts endemic to New York sidewalks, and went flying flat on his face.

Fancy Dancer

Slipping, sliding, rhythmically writhing on a scrap of linoleum unfurled beneath Times Square, just beyond the platform where the "S" Shuttle secretes its load of humanity, I witnessed a bone-thin man with jet black, slicked-back hair, whisk his willowy partner through a Latin dance routine.

Tipping and turning her tightly sheathed torso, he thrust a knee lasciviously between her pliant limbs for a torrid tango, the two of them practically going at it right then and there, when it suddenly dawned on me in an unsettling flash, that the dancer's partner was a doll, a skillfully stuffed appendage born of old socks and stifled libido.

Unabashed, the artificial duo strutted their stuff for the catcalling crowd. Several questions begged asking. How long have they been an item and an act? Were there earlier incarnations? (Fred Astaire famously tripped the light fantastic on screen with a compliant mop, Gene Kelley waltzed a wet umbrella.) How, where, when was such an astonishing spectacle first conceived and received? Were he/they applauded, taunted, jeered, assaulted in some smoky back room in Buenos Aires? Did a scandalized undercover man of the cloth stride forward and tear the tenuous twosome apart? Did the dancer secretly welcome the attack, not as a violation, but, rather, as a violent affirmation of his art?

Here is my theory. Seeing his sister-self in shreds, he cried and cursed him/them-self/selves at having gone public. But later, years later, in a single-room-occupancy hotel in Spanish Harlem, his partner was reborn, more radiant than ever, red-cheeked, drenched in cheap perfume, a plastic rose planted in her tightly braided hair, henceforth to tour the underground platforms of this world with him — in flagrant duality — and one day, perhaps, if the mood is right, to conceive a dancing heir!

Restless Metal Steps

In childhood, I liked to ride escalators backwards, scaling the downward rush. I have since tried them all, from the historic shuffling wooden clip-clop at Macy's, the first building in the world to be so endowed, in 1902, to my favorite, the restless metal steps clawing their way into the bedrock underground Grand Central Station, linking the platform of the Number-7 Flushing Line to the Number-6 Lexington Line. The steep diagonal angle of entry confounds the predictable horizontal and vertical coordinates of urban life; rollercoaster-like precisely because it confounds and because you know the confusion is short-lived, it draws you into a dreamlike state of dizziness in which individuality dissolves into liquid motion. The escalator does the rushing for you, and so, paradoxically, suspends all haste. Teeth clenched, chafing at the bit, these tireless mechanical pack mules scale and descend the dizzying diagonal bluff day and night without so much as a whinny of complaint. And if you're lucky you'll be serenaded below, as I was, by a harpist plucking the theme song from *The Godfather*.

Attached Twins

"WALK!" invites the kindly little white manikin. "DON'T WALK!" commands his malevolent red brother, a menacing right hand held aloft. One the personification of YES, the other NO incarnate. How can they stomach such close confinement without tearing each other to shreds? What unimaginable miseries must they suffer in silence, never, the one or the other, able to completely be himself, boxed unborn in that electric limbo! For what can stopping mean to a homunculus who has never known motion? And how, on the other hand, without ever having taken a single step forward, can his counterpart put himself in the shoes of one impatient to proceed? Never to indulge your deepest desire to let yourself go! Crossed purposes permit them no more than a titillating blink at each alternating turn of the tide. What if the two were actually a Jekyll-Hyde composite of incompatible impulses bottled up in one and the same bosom! Put yourself in their place! What can it cost, in any case, to consider their lot and sympathize en route, while waiting for the light to change?

Deadhouse

Frenetic hoop shooters dribble and shoot and diehard handball players hammer the walls at the basketball and handball courts on the corner of Sixth Avenue and West Third Street. Aficionados flock by to catch class acts at the Blue Note, the big-time jazz club down the block. And depending on the hour, the McDonald's across the street attracts a steady stream of college students, tourists, junkies, insomniacs, and beggars freshly flush with change. But there is something about the narrow green nook that deflects attention.

Presently occupied by a nondescript 7-Eleven store, it was in previous incarnations an all-day breakfast and bagels place, a pharmacy, and an Italian trattoria that swapped its "Grand Opening" banner for an "Under New Management" sign less than six months after opening. The new management never materialized.

I could have told them not to bother! Years ago, a woman was murdered on the premises.

I don't really believe in ghosts, but once at the end of a gray, rainy day, round about twilight, I emerged umbrella-less in a downpour from the subway station on the corner, intending to make a beeline for the abandoned doorway. The rain kept changing direction from a vertical incision to a dizzy diagonal, sounding off like eggs sizzling on the sidewalk. The building was boarded up.

As I was about to run for cover, I spotted a woman huddling in the doorway with a red silk scarf looped loosely around her neck bending over to straighten a sagging black fishnet stocking. Propriety should have compelled me to look away, still I let my gaze linger. A big mistake in the City, where mishaps are waiting to happen. Just then a white stretch limousine, one of those elongated lizards that transport party animals around town, drove by and splashed me with filthy water from a curbside puddle. I wiped my face and when I looked up the woman was gone.

Call me a fool, but I don't think that any enterprise will ever survive and prosper at that spot.

Wall Street in Diapers

There is an undeniable similarity between corporate boardrooms and daycare centers. Both have big tables and easels beset with illustrated large-lettered educational displays designed to placate investors in the first instance and parents in the second, both of whom have provided the seed money with high hopes for the growth of their investment. The fact that CEOs and chairmen of the board are given to temper tantrums and get driven around like the baby carriage contingent merely proves my point.

Giving the Finger

To the left of the Temple of Dendur, in the Egyptian wing of the Metropolitan Museum of Art, there is a depot of preserved body parts. When the display first opened, I noticed a mummified finger sequestered away on a lower shelf. On a subsequent visit the finger was gone. The number to call for inquiries is 212-879-5500, ext. 3770. Being civically minded — the historic finger is, after all, public property! — I called to report its absence, but have yet to receive a reply. Meanwhile in a nearby cabinet languishes a mummified liver. Actually, according to the label, it's "an organ, probably a liver," they're not exactly sure. You'd think they ought to know by now!

Handle as Luggage

Waiting for a flight out of La Guardia Airport, I was somewhat disconcerted by the spectacle of a passenger stepping off the plane, just in from Houston, clutching a cardboard box marked: HUMAN EYES, with a red sticker marked: HANDLE AS LUGGAGE!

Assessing Antiques

The mint quality Louis XVI bureau on which President Kennedy signed the nuclear test ban treaty with the Russians in 1963 was sold at auction at Sotheby's some years ago for $1.43 million. A bit pricey, I find, for a piece of furniture on which one man rested his elbow and signed his name a single time. Me too, I'm thinking of auctioning off my old writing table, a vintage Downtown diner Formica counter top, circa 1960, retrieved from the street. The petrified chewing gum wads stuck under it are guaranteed 100% authentic, glued there by taxi and truck drivers, cashiers, poets, prostitutes, insomniacs of every ilk, desperate and anonymous, stretching a single cup of coffee to slow down the frenetic passage of time. I am willing to accept any and all reasonable offers, screws and stains included.

The City That Never Sleeps

They call it "the city that never sleeps," but New York dreams round the clock of a hot tip at the racetrack or breakfast at Tiffany's! It flashes its assets and almost immediately thereafter erases the lewd revelation. It vaunts its grandeur and spits on the reflection. Manhattan marvels at and mocks itself in the same breath. They spray-paint new installments of commentary wherever space permits. Realtors grasp everything by day. At night, the City belongs to the tireless army of muralists, scribblers, and posterers, in the morning the clean-up crew scrape it clean. The murmuring walls are a tabula rasa, perpetually revised, a magic slate offering the instant satisfaction of doing and undoing.

A Last One-Liner

What did the Zen master say to the New York hotdog vendor? "Make me one with everything!"

Never Mind the Notes, Just Worry 'bout the Chords 'n Intervals

"If you have to ask what jazz is, you'll never know."

— Louis Armstrong

At the time I fancied myself a budding talent, though I'd have been hard pressed to say at what. Singer-songwriter was my latest label, only I sang mostly in the shower and could never quite manage, once toweled dry, to make the plucked strings accord with the words. My lessons with a lovely, dark-eyed guitarist of Hungarian extraction were going nowhere. Every week she chided me with a fiery, Magyar-accented intensity for not practicing enough, and every week I promised to apply myself, but if truth be told, I was far more interested in playing her heartstrings than the catgut of my guitar, and made no headway in either endeavor.

The lessons let out at twilight, when the setting sun spreads mystery or menace, depending on the neighborhood and your state of mind.

Formerly bordering on Tin Pan Alley, the popular music Mecca where aspiring songwriters like Irving Berlin made their mark, the enclave of townhouses and apartment buildings comprising Murray Hill, on the western rim of Manhattan's East Side, was more recently redubbed "Curry Hill" on account of the profusion of South Asian restaurants that nowadays fill up at dinnertime with hungry young professionals. But in the late Seventies, when the encounter I am about to relate took place, the neighborhood was in sad decline, frequented mostly, come nightfall, by pimps, prostitutes, and their prospective clientele.

Unattached at the time, and in no great hurry to get home, I dragged my feet, letting my battered guitar case knock against my knees, taking timid sidelong looks at the scantily clad ladies of the night, as I rounded the corner of Lexington and 25th, past the faded façade of the 69th Regiment Armory, the site of the legendary Armory Art Show of 1913, where Marcel Duchamp's "Nude Descending a Staircase, No. 2" caused a stir, taking the staid American art scene by storm. But like the neighborhood, the armory, too, had seen better days, its shadowy external alcoves now haunted by hookers and pushers. Tin Pan Alley, the Armory Art Show, Irving Berlin, and Marcel Duchamp all belonged to the long ago. Why, I wondered, did nothing of note ever happen in my time?

So when a tall, thin man leaning in one such nook, muttered something, a come-on, I presumed, I didn't give it another thought. But when he stepped toward me out of the shadow, I froze in fear, with my feet facing forward and head twisted back, squeezing the handle of the guitar case in a futile attempt to get a grip on myself, or if need be, to wield as a weapon. It was his words, repeated a second time and enunciated clearly, that really took me by surprise. "Never mind the notes," he said, "just worry 'bout the chords 'n intervals!"

Struck dumb, I stared back.

"Relax, I ain't goin' to mug you!" He tittered through the gaps between two broken top teeth. "You ain't never goin' to make music all twisted up like some damn circus monkey!"

I did indeed feel at that moment like a cymbal-striking mechanical monkey with a broken coil, a malfunctioning wind-up toy from my childhood. But how did he know?

"You are where you are," he shrugged, "ain't no place no time but here 'n now!"

I continued to stare back, bewildered.

"Listen," he said, launching into a story. "Back in the Fifties, when th' only place white 'n black ever crossed paths was on the keyboard, the chessboard, or at the morgue, this white chick stuck around for my last set, always the best, at the club I was playin' at in The Village." (He lowered his gaze, turning the derision inwards.) "Fool that I am, a proper gen'l'man, like my mama raised me, I was walkin' this white chick I wa'n't even into down Mulberry Street in Li'l Italy, which ain't no place for no black man to be walkin' no white chick, never mind the time o' day, when this big gorilla comes chargin' out of a doorway, holdin' a hatchet like he's meanin' to subdivide my *real* estate split level-wise. — 'Hold it, Sal!' she shrieks, 'it ain't like that!' — Then he snorts, like I seen this bull do one time back when me 'n the band toured Spain, 'fore he gored a matador in the groin. — Wingtips primed for take-off, my shoes was stuck to the ce-ment, 'n all I could do 's look 'im in the eye 'n whisper what, I swear to God, I believed was gonna be my last words: 'Honest, Mister, I'm just walkin' the lady home!' — Then the gorilla grunts somethin' 'n lowers the axe. Maybe he's still mad, maybe he's glad, beats me. Breathless, I haul ass back to my pad uptown, belt down a fifth o' Johnny Walker Black, bang on the keyboard to stop my fingers from tremblin', 'n riff out my first hit tune." (He hummed a few bars, before bursting into a raspy smoker's cough, and gave up.) — "And that, son, is the secret of improvisation! Don't never be afraid to fumble, 'cause that's where the music is!"

I sensed that I was in the presence of a master. He might have been famous, for all I knew. His gaunt cheeks were covered with a several days' growth of gray stubble, long before it was fashionable. His life, he let slip, was out of whack. — "I tickle them keys, but they don't sing to me no more."

Neither of us felt a pressing need to do anything or be anyplace else, so we bought a couple of beers and squatted on the uncomfortable narrow stoop surrounding the rim of Gramercy Park, the last gated enclave in the city, watching a solitary old man in a wheelchair, with a sour-faced nurse seated on the bench beside him in silence, both staring into the void.

"Like some fancy-ass prison for millionaires!" he squelched a chuckle.

I held back a laugh.

"What you up to, son?" he asked.

"Kind of in between things at the moment," I allowed.

He looked me in the eye. — "You alone, I can smell it!"

Again, I was taken aback. How did he know?!

"Ain't no shame in bein' alone!" He smiled like he knew the score. "It's a time to retune your instrument!"

"Will do!" I said, tapping my guitar case.

"It ain't up to *you!*" he gave me another laser look. "Man likes to think he's callin' the shots, but it's always the lady that leads. You been lookin' too hard! Let *her* find *you!*"

(It would be another couple of years until I happened to chat up a petite brunette at a party. *She* called *me* up a week later, and we've been married ever since. But that's another story.)

Just then a passing policeman rapped his nightstick against a "No Loitering" sign. We had already drained our beers and tossed the cans in the trash, or else we would certainly have had trouble.

The pianist and the policeman exchanged wary looks, even as the latter continued on his beat.

My man fell silent. "So long!" he said as soon as the cop was out of sight. Before I could respond he disappeared and we returned to our separate destinies.

*

Skip a decade. It's late. I'm dashing uptown to Babies Hospital at Columbia-Presbyterian, where my daughter has just been born. The A-Train, that winged subterranean Pegasus that leaps in a single bound from 59th Street and Columbus Circle all the way up to 125th Street in Harlem, is whisking me up to Washington Heights in a heartbeat. Oblivious to time and place, I am whistling to myself the jazz standard "Take the A Train," when the well-dressed, middle-aged man seated directly opposite me breaks into a smile.

"Ellington really taps the sound of the City!" I smile back.

"Ellington didn't write it," he protests, "the score's by Billy Strayhorn, 'n I damn well ought to know, 'cause he was my uncle."

*

Post Script. I've been married for three decades and counting. We give each other room to dream. I still sing in the shower when nobody's listening. But as it turned out, I didn't have the chops for a musician, and passed my instrument on to my son, born five years later, who really knows how to make the strings sing. Stringing words together is my thing. I keep listening for life's resounding chords and intervals.

Hizzoner Waves

His great hand keeps waving interminably in memory like the wobbly fin of an animated fish — a shark, a dolphin, or a great white whale, or the paw-waving golden fortune cat in Chinese restaurants — from a motorboat weaving its way among the pleasure crafts anchored in the Easter River in eager anticipation of the fireworks display. (It is in the waning hours of the Fourth of July, in 1985.) I spot Hizzoner himself, the late, in every way larger than life Ed Koch, the 105th mayor of the City of New York, then running for reelection for a third term, bobbing into view, calling out to the crowd. A New York fixture, in his day he was practically as anchored in the city's imagination as the memory of King Kong clinging to the spire of the Empire State Building.

Elsewhere people tend to emphasize the welfare of the interlocutor over that of the self, to wit: "How are *you* doing?" But this is, after all, New York, a place so consumed by self-importance, its residents refer to it as *The* City, as if there were no other. And this is Mayor Koch, the towering one-man skyscraper and living embodiment of The City's unabashed narcissism, cementing his place in local lore between the second shortest and first full-fledged Jewish mayor, Abe Beam, and the first black mayor, David Dinkins.

"How'm *I* doin'?" Koch calls out, a catchphrase that echoes the collective solipsism that has congealed around him — the image of a giant man o' war jellyfish comes to mind — seeing itself reflected in his wobbly image, and handily sweeping him into office for a third tenure.

Robbing the Seagulls of Their Virgin Shriek

I did not come to Cape Cod intending to write about it. Quite the contrary, it seemed to me that ever since Henry David Thoreau's account posthumously published in 1865, the Cape had become a travel cliché combed by naturalists and novelists, trampled by summer hordes, and done to death by gossip columnists and paparazzi tracking the Kennedy clan. But that magical juncture of sand, sea, and sky where Massachusetts curls its salty tongue out into the Atlantic took me by surprise, casting its unshakable spell, compelling tribute.

The journalistic business that brought me to Osterville (a posh pocket of blue blood gentility at Mid Cape) having been completed, I hightailed it up Route 6 to Wellfleet on the Outer Cape. The idea was to take a solitary stroll on the beach, a whiff of salt sea air and a bowl of clam chowder. Little did I suspect that it would be love at first breath of the Cape Cod National Seashore, a 40-mile stretch of unspoiled beachhead from Chatham to Provincetown designated a protected area by Hyannis homeboy President John F. Kennedy in 1961.

Rising like a great fist of sand, a contrecoup to the restless onslaught of the foamy deep, the 65-foot dune at Cahoon Hollow Beach off Ocean View Drive in Wellfleet whopped me right in the solar plexus. Weaving and waltzing, the Atlantic Ocean followed with a hard right. All I could do was gaze and gasp. Though the beach grass was still blue-green, the air had a crisp autumnal nip. It was late September and the summer crowds were long gone, leaving behind a lone fisherman and a kid flying his kite. I took off my shoes, slid barefoot down the dune and walked along the winding beachhead till a bend in the sand swallowed fisherman and kid. I sat down and watched a bobbing black spot in the foam where the gulls circled low. It might or might not have been a seal. Lacking binoculars, I had to make do with the naked eye.

Back in town, the desolation was likewise soothing. Off-season Wellfleet retains the sleepy air of the New England fishing village it once was. Even Main Street, with its sprinkling of galleries, boutiques, and restaurants (most closed till next summer) invites a quiet stroll. Left to your own devices, a little imagination will fill in the gaps. You can get a cup of coffee and browse the holdings of local talent at the public library.

The erstwhile home of poet Edna St. Vincent Millay and the scene of sometime resident Mary McCarthy's roman à cléf, A Charmed Life, Wellfleet confirmed its literary heritage in a chance encounter. They'd been digging up the roadbed near a high-end thrift shop called Eccentricity. Waiting in my car to be waved on by a policeman posted at the site, I noticed an old man with a white shaggy mane and bushy eyebrows at the wheel of the car waiting to pass in the opposite direction. His intense gull-like gaze briefly interlocked with mine. The face looked familiar. "You can go now, Norman!" said the young woman seated beside him. It might or might not have been the late novelist Norman Mailer.

Allergic to the crowd, yet determined to make it to the tip of the Cape, the next morning I drove with a lingering dread the 14 miles north to Provincetown, expecting to find a raucous honky-tonk town. But except for a busload of snap-shooting souvenir hunters rubbing elbows with purple-haired nose-ringed locals on Commercial Street, off-season P-town proved a pretty peaceful place. The Pilgrims first landed here in 1620 (before pushing on to Plymouth Rock), and Portuguese fishermen subsequently cast their nets. They were followed in the 20th century by dramatist Eugene O'Neil and succeeding generations of Greenwich Village writers and artists and denizens of every stripe who set the tolerant tone of anything-goes. The mood holds off-season as well as on-, but the decibel level and body count are considerably lower after Labor Day.

I dutifully climbed the Pilgrim Monument on High Pole Hill, all 353 feet of it above sea level, for a sweeping bayside view of Long Point Light and the busy barnacle cluster clam bed of cottages comprising downtown.

But feeling reclusive and wanting to take in a surfeit of sea and dunes in my brief stay, I fled to Herring Cove Beach at the edge of town and walked its length to Race Point Light, following in the footsteps of Thoreau. In season, I understand, this sheltered stretch of dramatic sunsets is the unspoken preserve of same-sex couples. Off-season, it was pretty much me and the gulls nesting noisily along the shore.

The mood was a salty blend of Autumnal melancholy, the ocean and sky being a gray shade of blue, with the shrub oak and wild plum so prized by Thoreau streaked squash yellow and cranberry red by the freewheeling hand of nature. Driftwood bleached a ghostly white lay about like whale bones on the beach. An occasional whitecap blossomed like a forget-me-not on the flat blue lawn of Massachusetts Bay.

The dunes are lower here than in Wellfleet, but they spread across the interior, walling in the salt pond habitats of wild ducks and loons.

A sinking feeling of despair — before the advent of the digital camera — when my old Minolta ran out of film at the crest of a dune, soon succumbed to a profound relief. No longer obliged to distance myself behind a 35-mm lens, I had no recourse but to join nature, to let the naked eye cavort with the windy clash of sand and sea and inhale the vapor of creation.

I admit to feeling a tinge of guilt at robbing the seagulls of their virgin shriek and subjugating life to language. But oohs and ahs do not suffice before such windswept majesty. Even a loner like Thoreau felt compelled to put his wonderment into words. He filled a book-length manuscript with observations and reflections of a mere several weeks' looking. I figured I could legitimately extract a few reflections out of a long weekend on the Cape.

New Orleans Reveries

This tribute to the Big Easy was composed by an adoring admirer from the Big Apple, who has on occasion fled south to elude whatever ails him, and to indulge a weakness for oysters, stories, and romance.

Oysters

"Oysters, I tell you, it's true," the man with the walrus mustache insists, lapping up the last succulent morsel of salty flesh, tipping the shell to his whiskered lips.

It is lunchtime, some years ago, and K-Paul's Kitchen, the reputed New Orleans eatery, then just recently opened for business, is already packed, obliging hungry gourmets to double up at table. No matter. Delights of the palate are best enjoyed in company. Satisfied tongues slip easily into conversation.

The man's story, true or not, is vintage New Orleans, as steeped in romance as the bread pudding we both order for dessert is steeped in rum.

"Great Great Great Granddaddy, God rest his feisty soul," the man relates, "was quite the Casanova of his little Norman village. The youngest son of an aristocratic family of declined means, he hunted skirts for sport. Sex was his elixir, kept him young well into his nineties.

"Dallying one night with the Countess So and So, he was rudely interrupted by an irate Count.

"'Excusez moi!' my ancestor, a man of impeccable manners,

exclaimed, and lacking time enough to pull on his pants, leaped forthwith out the window, barely eluding a bullet aimed at his heart, climbed down a fortuitously situated vine, and ran naked into the night, from whence, with the aid of family and friends, he made his way to New Orleans."

Mary's Snowball

Capital of eccentricity, haven of the odd, New Orleans is pure story, a narrative forever unraveling on the lips of its loquacious citizens, in the still-life pantomime of its aging façades.

Here a shabby liquor store in a rundown tenement district dubs itself the House of Joy, and a taxi driver weaves parable out of a banal exchange on the weather.

"It snowed once fifty years ago," the driver, a gray-haired Cajun, replies to a passenger's idle inquiry about the weather. "A few flakes is all, melted just as soon as it hit the ground, but Mary Rooney rushed out with a spoon and scraped up a snowball, the only one of its kind in the entire state of Louisiana. She was a popular girl after that. Kept it in the icebox, displayin' it on rare occasions to the boys she took a fancy to. 'I saw it,' the boys'd boast, 'I saw Mary's Snowball.' Kept it frozen up and ready for her weddin' day, when she proudly presented it along with the embroidered sheets to the man of her choosin'. 'It's yours now, honey,' she said, whippin' open the icebox door..."

The Columns

The Columns Hotel, an antebellum mansion on St. Charles Avenue in the Garden District, is named for the two neoclassical pillars that adorn the lower tier of its front porch, supporting the upper level.

Vibrations from the St. Charles Line, one of the only street-cars still in service (Desire having long since been replaced by a bus), punctuate the silence by day; and crickets jam non-stop through the languid summer night.

This gallant structure, which stands removed from the activity of the street by a width of un-groomed weed and dusty earth, boasts in its interior a splendid winding oaken stairway topped by a stained-glass skylight in the shape of the sun, bathing the steps by day in a perpetual rainbow of light.

It is here that the late French film director Louis Malle shot *Pretty Baby*, his idyll to Storyville (New Orleans' famed red-light district, the cradle of jazz). On these steps, actress Brooke Shields made her adolescent debut as a succulent virgin served on a platter to a party of leering old roués.

Floorboards creak, doors rattle, hinges squeak, and the furnishings straddle the tenuous divide between antique and trash.

Take the furnishings of my room, for instance: Three monstrous mud-brown armoires of varying height and scratch-streaked finish; a table stabilized by a moldy wad of newsprint; a sink whose faucet functions fitfully and in gasps; and a Model-T air conditioner: a big black box balanced precariously just above the headboard of a tarnished brass bed.

The air conditioner, as opposed to the faucet, is unstoppable, its vintage motor blasting Arctic air night and day on the face of the defenseless sleeper.

Climactic Interlude

A fog is rising, spilling out over the muddy waters of the Mississippi, coating the air for miles about with an opaque curtain of mist.

I am walking home with a young woman, a fellow boarder at The Columns on St. Charles, through the lush verdure of the Garden District, where towering old oaks and magnolias caress the rooftops of run-down palatial estates.

It is past midnight and the streets are deserted, as far as I can tell.

The silence is thick and green, indistinguishable from the heavy air in which it floats, infused with the almost suffocating sweetness of magnolia.

We grope our way through the mist, the blind leading the blind. The street signs are out of eye-reach, and there is no way of telling for sure where we are. It is a comfort, under the circumstances, to trip over the familiar tracks of the St. Charles Line. It can't be much farther, I think. But it is. Distance swells in a green haze.

The atmosphere is pure gothic, only the danger-music is missing. I can feel the first flutter of trepidation in the pit of my stomach, but at this early stage it is only a tickle, an occasional palpitation. I can sense that my companion feels it too by the stiff way she walks, but having only just met her I am reticent to reach for her hand. She is blonde and tall and comes from Kansas.

"Two of my favorite books take place in Kansas," I say, to make conversation, "*The Wizard of Oz* and *In Cold Blood*."

She makes no reply, and I realize, too late, that my mention of the latter title was ill-timed, under the circumstances.

A traffic light blinks like a nervously twitching eye overhead. The absence of traffic or other pedestrians makes the light appear ludicrous, an archaic remnant of a bygone era of visibility.

The green disc turns bloodshot red.

Boldly, nevertheless, I step forward, feeling the curb retreat beneath my feet as I sink into the tarry blacktop softened by the sun.

Then out of nowhere, a voice, slow, ominous, and clipped, commands: "Don't cross at the red light!"

I look up with a start, and vaguely decipher the outline of a parked patrol car off to my right.

A match is struck. I hear it and see the flicker, the grinning face of a man lighting a cigarette flashes and fades at the wheel.

Local Fauna

Rooms being cheap, The Columns attracts a varied and colorful clientele.

Consider the couple from Bensonhurst.

Jim takes pictures, Desirée poses in dishabille, though it is hard to imagine what he sees in her.

The strap of her graying slip is forever falling off at the bony shoulder, its hem peeking out from under the shapeless black shift she wears in public. Such habits of dress might be enticing, but Desirée's anorexic stare and skeletal torso confound desire. Still Jim dotes on her, convinced that every man would pounce if he had the chance.

They came to Louisiana looking for spiders and snakes to add to their live collection back home in Brooklyn.

"Avachnids," says Desirée, who likes to be photographed with a black widow running up her leg, "ahr vewy sensual, ya know."

Desirée—as Rémy, the night clerk at The Columns confesses one evening over a joint of Jamaican—is a veritable spider under the sheets.

Rémy's face, like rawhide, weathered and abused, is still resilient at 42, still open to the unexpected. His droopy eyes fasten on the joint we are passing as on a minuscule prey he might at any moment pounce on and devour.

"You remind me," I say (in the unhinged way marijuana loosens the lips) "of the lizards I saw in Pompeii perched like spirits of the dead on the walls of ruined villas in the dust of incinerated souls, sizing up the living."

Rémy takes a long, deep toke, gulps down the pungent smoke like it was a shot of bourbon (his preferred intoxicant), and laughs a slow, considered laugh. "I knew a fellah once," he says, returning the shuttlecock of the absurd, "crowed like a rooster every time he spotted a lady he liked." Rémy demonstrates. (His rooster is less convincing than his lizard though. We are all born with a certain spirit, it seems, and cannot swap it for another.) "He was one wired rooster," says Rémy, "just out of the pen, where he done time for cutting up a chicken hawk — that rooster was hungry for chickens, roast, stewed or fricasseed, any way you like. We took him along on a sandblastin' job just out of Centreville, to help him get re-accustomed to freedom. You ever been to Centreville? No?

There ain't much to it really, just one long main street with a bar at one end and another at th' other.

"Six hours sandblastin' is like twelve hours of anything else. Pays good money though, but it makes you awful thirsty. The first bar's closed, so we head for the second, which is not much different from the first: a straight, long, wood counter, like a shrunken miniature main street. Well there's three men standin' at one end of the bar and two women sittin' at th' other, so you know which end we picked.

"Rooster takes a shine to a little blonde vacuum-packed into a pair o' jeans, and he starts crowin' sunrise. She smiles. He says, 'How 'bout a beer?' Next thing you know a man from the far end comes amblin' over, whips out a pistol, and holds it to the back o' Rooster's head. He says, 'How'd you like to die!'

"'Well,' says Rooster, turnin' slow 'n easy, his nose to the nozzle, 'if it's gotta be, it's gotta be.' And he starts laughin' like it's the funniest joke he ever heard.

"The bar goes stone silent. All you hear is Rooster's cocka-mamie laugh.

"'I tell you what,' he says, his chest still heavin' with hilarity, 'Why don't you go ahead 'n shoot me!'

"'You wanna die so bad!?' says the man with the pistol.

"'Shoot me!' Rooster shouts, spins off the barstool, wrestles the piece out of the man's hand, and points it at his head. 'I think I might shoot you!' he says, the laughter drained from his lips.

"I swear," says Rémy, "the silence was so loud you could hear it thump!"

"Then Rooster, he turns to the barman, slaps a twenty down on the counter, cracks a cagy smile. 'Beers all around,' he says, sending the pistol sliding down the polished wood like a shuffle puck.

"'Here's to Centreville!' he says, raising his glass," and simultaneous with the telling, Rémy takes another toke.

R.S.V.P.

"You *will* be back for the party, won't you!" the night clerk calls to me.

I am on my way out to prowl the Quarter, but impatience succumbs to curiosity: "What party?"

"You mean you haven't been invited!" says Rémy, his brow raised in amazement. He watches me, savoring my chagrin just long enough before blurting out: "O' course you're invited! Everyone's invited! It's Mrs. Moore's birthday, her sixtieth, and don't be late! She don't take kindly to tardiness!"

"Who the devil is Mrs. Moore!?"

The night clerk chuckles. Being privy to the comings and goings-on at The Columns, he relishes the relative power of his position. The night is his domain. The front door being locked after midnight, he will sometimes leave a guest who forgot the key waiting and ringing for a quarter of an hour or more just to tease, before he saunters over to release the latch with a shrug of feigned annoyance. As annoyed as you may be, you can hardly hold it against him. It is just one of his many games to keep himself entertained through the interminable stretch of his nocturnal vigil.

"Nine o'clock sharp!" he says, with a sly grin. "She'll want you to look into her mirror, of course."

"Of course," I reply, not wanting to be made a fool of, "me 'n Snow White," convinced that Mrs. Moore's a bit of Picayune lore, a dowager ghost, or x-rated Storyville specter. "I'll be sure to bring along the seven dwarves too," I add, slipping out into the night in search of distraction.

Through the Looking Glass

"You're late," says the night clerk, "follow me!"

Strangers are rushing past us, some barefoot, some in sandals, some in sequined high heels up the winding oaken steps, past a sign on the wall of the second floor, above a red velvet cord symbolically barring the way to the third: BEWARE OF GREY BEAR!

Rémy ceremoniously unclasps the cord and refastens it behind us.

He knocks at a door at the head of the stairs, the only accessible door (the others are blocked up by heaps of furniture in various states of disrepair). We are ushered in by a big Black woman with quiet magisterial dignity and a crushed pumpkin face.

"That's Rose," says Rémy, who melts back into the throng of guests.

I am left standing alone, overwhelmed and a little intimidated by the splendor of the premises and the motley mix of the crowd.

Starlets and spinsters, gentlemen in smoking jackets and punks in tattered jeans mingle amicably in a lavish green velvet wallpapered salon, its high ceiling hung with crystal chandeliers, its floor covered with a vast, predominantly red patterned oriental rug. At a grand piano situated roughly in the center of the room, a barefoot figure sits shirtless, crooning love songs with a Liberace lilt.

And just as I consider making a hasty departure, the sea of humanity opens to make way for a tall, gaunt, gray-haired lady in a floor length, emerald-studded satin gown, supported at either elbow by Rémy and Rose.

"Hi, I'm Lee Moore," she says, extending a bony white hand. "Rémy tells me you've a lively imagination."

"If he says so," I nod.

"Well then, you simply must have a look at my mirror."

She beckons; I follow behind, an obedient, if somewhat disoriented Alice in the thrall of the indomitable Queen of Hearts.

Rémy and Rose propel the old woman through the throng, down an endless corridor, the walls of which are dotted with memorabilia: A black and white glossy of an enticing teenage Mary Tyler Moore in a cheesecake pose, signed "To Aunt Lee, with love"; a page of sheet music inscribed with Victor Borge's black bow tie insignia; and framed letters from Richard Nixon and H.R. Haldeman thanking her for her hospitality.

"There," she says, pointing an imperious finger at a pane of barely reflective glass, set in a recess in the wall, its streaked and mottled surface blackened with age. Below it, on an antique coffee table supported by lion's paws, lies a Moroccan red leather-bound tome with an owl on the cover.

"You look, and write down what you see," Rémy whispers.

Is this some joke or a time-honored ritual?

I peer into the black surface and see nothing but a chaos of dots, streaks and splotches. Mrs. Moore is waiting. I look again, still nothing. In fairy tales the image appears instantly, reality takes time. Rémy passes me a joint to spark the imagination. I take a hit and stare. I want to see something, for politeness sake. Little by little the mirror gets cooking, the splotches leap agitatedly about. I open the book and duly write down, inspired by a legendary figure I'd recently read about:

"Olivia, the Oyster Dancer (bona fide Storyville star who could shimmy an oyster all over her naked body, no kidding! and never let it drop)."

I take a minute to leaf through the pages and peruse the other visions, and discover the following entry to my great surprise and delight: "Oh honey, don't let me commence!" signed with a hasty scrawl, Truman Capote.

"I'm in good company," I say, turning to my hostess, but find myself alone in an empty corridor.

Down the hall, meanwhile, the party is in full swing.

Mrs. Moore holds court in a red velvet Louis XVI chair, a settee of the king who lost his head.

"Aspirin," says a young woman sucking on an unlit Virginia Slim, "is the best form of birth control. You hold the pill between your bare knees and never let go."

"But thatth no fun, ith it," the piano player protests, and shifting repertoire, hammers and howls: "Ah can't get no oh tha-tith-fac-thun, and ah try, and ah try, and ah try, and ah try..."

A monster of a long-haired Himalayan cat with orange

bloodshot eyes waddles over, swinging a huge furry tail, toppling drinks off of tables onto the oriental rug. The cat curls up at Mrs. Moore's spindly ankles.

"Now now, Grey Bear," says Mrs. Moore, half scolding, half cooing with affection, bending over to pet it.

"Go ahead, coddle the beast," says Rose, "I'm the one that's gotta clean up after her!"

"I know," says Mrs. Moore, "I spoil her something awful. Poor baby, my kitty cat prefers bourbon to milk."

"The bitch just can't hold her liquor!" Rose fumes.

"Like somebody else I know," replies Mrs. Moore.

"Like who!?" Rose tilts back her pumpkin face and folds her flabby arms in a formidable physical challenge.

"Aw hell, I'm just kidding, ya big brown tub o' molasses!" says Mrs. Moore.

The showdown dissolves in laughter. The look exchanged belies a secret understanding. This is the squabble of intimates, not the colloquy of mistress and maid.

"When I met Rose," Mrs. Moore avows for the benefit of all present, "I learned to laugh again. Look what she gave me for my birthday." She plucks a charm necklace from around her neck. "With my money, I might add!" Three gold hearts dangle from the chain, on each a different word inscribed. Mrs. Moore reads aloud: "Live! ... Love! ... Laugh! ... And that's just what I plan to do for the rest of my days..."

The tail end of a conversation catches my ear.

"Splendid hostess! Remember the garden party she gave in '65? Her fourth husband Lambert had just laid out a layer of cement in the patio. 'Is it dry yet, darling?' he asked, skimming the surface with the tip of his little finger. 'Let's see," she says, tears open her blouse and presses her boobs into the still soft cement, and let me tell you, they made quite an impression. 'No,' she says, 'still wet.'"

The Spirit of Water

Overshadowed by the portraits of New Orleans notables, Faro, the spirit of water, huddles in a glass case in a hidden corner of the New Orleans Museum of Art, far from his native Niger River.

This beady-eyed, red African idol holds sway in some mysterious way over that human gumbo, that peculiar confluence of populations (African, Indian, Spanish, French, Irish, and a little bit of everything else) that settled along the lip of land where the Mississippi spits into the sea.

Here sweet and salty, crayfish and shrimp, alligator and oyster, mix.

Here the clash of African and Caucasian makes unforgettable blue music.

Like an African Pinocchio, this brooding, seething puppet reveals a subliminal secret: red female breasts sprout out of his black male torso.

For Faro, omnipotent god of the Bozo tribe of Mali (as the card in the display case explains) is of both sexes, having impregnated himself to give birth to the two hermaphrodite twins who, in turn, gave birth to humanity.

A prototypical New Orleans tale.

I hear the falsetto spirit of Truman Capote animating

Faro's wooden jaw, rattling the teeth, making bittersweet blue music for chameleons.

Till Death Do Us Part in the Delta:
A Mississippi Odyssey

Morgan City, Mississippi — The Delta isn't pretty by picture postcard standards. Desolation and despair lick every stick and brick of human habitation. Creeping vines choke abandoned shacks, the tendrils of nature reclaiming the detritus of culture. The suffocating flatness stretches as far as the eye can see. It's a lonesome lick of land that looks like it was lifted whole out of a parched African plain and dropped in Mississippi by mistake.

But the swamps wear a haunting iridescent coat of green, and even in late November, unpicked cotton balls dangle in the fields like orphaned slow flakes. Churned up by the foaming mouths of the Yazoo and Mississippi rivers, this soggy triangle effused the Blues, that bittersweet blend of half-remembered griot chants and plantation field hollers filtered through the parched throats and plucked on the broken heartstrings of the sons and daughters of slaves. A moaned anthem of survival, whetted with whiskey, lust, anger, anguish and longing, the Blues are the half-brother of Jazz and granddaddy of Rock 'n Roll, and, arguably, America's greatest homegrown musical gift to the world.

Driving through Morgan City — an abbreviated urban sprawl of bare cinder block dwellings and immobilized mobile homes that never quite got started — I pulled into a combination gas station-convenience store. Two bone-thin, old Black men sat out front gently rocking on straw settees not originally meant for motion. They suddenly stopped rocking and turned their heads as one, as I climbed out of the car, wary of my white face, like an invading chess piece from the far side of the board.

"Pardon me," I said, pained to be the cause of their distress, "I'm looking for the grave of Robert Johnson."

They stared back in stony silence, two black knights holding the fort.

"Ro-bert John-son," I enunciated clearly, lest my Yankee accent be the problem, "I heard he's buried hereabouts."

They looked me over hard and long. "You done come too late, Mister," the one with a tick in his right eye finally spoke up, "the hearse rolled by 'bout 'n hour ago."

I couldn't tell if I was being ribbed, riled or just plain misunderstood.

"You c'n try'n catch up with 'em at the graveyard if they ain't done diggin' yet, they dig slow in the Delta," the other man tried to console me.

"I don't believe we're talking about the same man," I said, choking back an involuntary chuckle.

"Ain't but one Robert Johnson in Morgan City," my first informant fired back, his right eye ticking up a storm, "'n he be bound for Kingdom Come by now!"

"I beg your pardon," I replied, "I mean the Bluesman who's been dead and gone for decades!"

At this point, a third man, who'd been listening in from behind a torn screen door, hollered: "I'll tell ya where he laid to rest, Mister, if you buy me a beer."

I was thirsty myself and happy to oblige with beers all

around.

"He a legend after his life!" the third man nodded.

I raised my can in a proposed toast: "To the King of the Delta Blues!"

"It be white man music now," he flashed me a canny cross between a chuckle and a smirk, "they done bleached out the black 'n milked out the blue." Laughter leaked through the gaps in his teeth. "But my man, he hoodwinked the Grim Reaper, split his self in two so nobody'd never track him down. They had to go 'n bury him twice."

The sun was sinking in the sky and Robert Johnsons were multiplying by the minute.

Finally fathoming whom I meant, the two men on the straw settees had a difference of opinion. The one with the tick in his right eye insisted he was buried "out by Mount Zion just up the road, not the first turn-off, but the second, betwixt the three-wheeled trailer and the tar-topped barn."

"As God is my witness," the second man solemnly shook his head, "his bones be laid to rest at the Payne Chapel Missionary Church in Quito."

Now the third man grinned triumphant: "Ain't none o' you knows the truth. He 'as poisoned back o' Three Forks to Quito, 'n funeralized at Payne Chapel alright, but his sistah, she had him dug up again 'n laid in at Mt. Zion, closer to home."

Reticent as I was to take sides, I only had time for one tomb.

Chasing the setting sun down Highway 7, as directed, turning right onto a nameless dirt road between the three-wheeled trailer and the tar-topped barn, I soon enough found Mount Zion Missionary Baptist Church, a little white clapboard chapel that rose suddenly out of the swamp. It was a peaceful last resting place for a man who had, according to legend, learned his guitar licks from the Devil himself, in exchange for his eternal soul.

I sat in the car, with a cd in the slot, and a recorded ghost growling, groaning, crooning and clowning, laughing at fortune and moaning at fate, mercilessly tickling guitar strings to a stride, strut, syncopated counterpoint or bottle-neck stride, as needed, more like a composite choir and band than a lonesome solo, singing:

"The blue-u-u-u-ues
is a low-down shakin' chill
You ain't never had 'em, I
hope you never will..."

I listened hard, trying to conjure up the face of that Black Rimbaud, narrating his own protracted season in hell:

"Umm mmm mmm mmm
blues fallin' down like hail
blues fallin' down like hail
And the days keeps on worryin' me
there's a hellhound on my trail
Hellhound on my trail..."

Lost in musical reverie, I didn't notice a car that pulled up alongside. — "You in any kind of trouble?" The young black man at the wheel, his wife beside him and two little boys in the back seat, all eyed me with a mix of curiosity and suspicion.

"I've come to pay my respects to the memory of a great

man," I said to set their minds at rest, remembering the unsolved rash of Black church burnings several summers ago.

"It's alright, Mister, you can go on in!" the driver nodded and drove off.

A gray granite obelisk, oddly Egyptian-looking for a cenotaph plunked in Mississippi mud, immediately stood out among the tombstones. Graced on one side with a grinning five and dime store snapshot, "You may bury my body/down by the highway side," it said on the second side; and the third was covered with the titles of songs listed in bold capital letters like great victories on a war memorial, which in a way they were, victories of the spirit: LOVE IN VAIN, LITTLE QUEEN OF SPADES, HELLHOUND ON MY TRAIL, ME AND THE DEVIL BLUES, et al.

I don't remember what it said on the fourth side. But behind the obelisk, a little off to the left, I noticed a freshly dug grave. Leaning in for a look, the somberness of the locale notwithstanding, I had to laugh. A hand-scrawled card on a pike identified the final resting place of Robert Johnson, the other Robert Johnson.

Tough Racket, Kid!

It is the summer of '82. I have just been laid off as an adjunct instructor of English composition at a second-rate college on Long Island where I might otherwise have languished in limbo for life, been jilted by a woman with a lingering stranglehold on my libido, and had a story rejected by the editor of a now defunct literary journal prominent at the time, whose precious boilerplate rejection letter began: "Yes, it is no, if you must know..." The play I've been struggling to write is stuck in stage directions. All of which I am stewing over when the telephone rings. It's my brother, my guardian angel when things are down. Having heard on the radio about an upcoming retrospective of the plays of Tennessee Williams at which the playwright himself would be present, at the summer theater festival in Williamstown, Massachusetts, he says: "Why don't you go?!"

It's a good five-hour bus ride from New York City Port Authority Bus Terminal to Williamstown. I am still traumatized by the six-hour bus ride I'd taken almost a decade before from Santillana del Mar in Spanish Basque country to the French border, suffering the adverse effects of a glass of unpasteurized milk unwisely imbibed to wash down a hunk of homemade cake, bought from two little old ladies tending a table just outside the Cave of Altamira, still open for public viewing back then. For six hours straight it felt like the horned bison and other creatures I'd seen painted by some prehistoric Picasso on rock were stampeding in my gut.

"Nowadays, American long-distance buses are all fitted

with functioning toilets!" my brother reassures me.

Once a way station on the Appalachian Trail, William-stown, the northwestern-most township in Massachusetts, is wedged up against the Vermont border and ringed by the Taconic Range of the Berkshires. Ranked among "The 100 Best Small Towns in America," it is home to the elite, button-down Williams College, founded in 1793. Launched in 1955, the annual Williamstown Summer Theatre Festival was then and still is going strong, last I heard.

I check into a nondescript motel and amble over to the festival box office. Tickets are still available for opening night. But living as I do on a shoestring, having set aside the neces-sary funds for a single night's lodging, a couple of beers, and the bus ride back home, I inadvertently neglected to allot the admission price to a single play.

Camped out at a bar with a bird's eye view of the theater, I munch on peanuts and nurse a single beer, pondering my options. The petite brunette barmaid is patient and pretty, a rare combination, and the bar is otherwise empty. I notice people pouring out of the theater at intermission time, which gives me an idea. Making sure that the box office is closed and the ticket takers have decamped, I bid the barmaid farewell, leave a dollar tip, which is all I have left, and mingle with the crowd milling about, following them back in for the second act.

The second-half of the opening-night program comprises a medley of moments from Williams' best-known works, featuring the actress Carrie Nye as an anorexic and deeply disturbed Blanche DuBois staggering down the stairs, certi-fiably well beyond the kindness of strangers, in the climactic scene of *A Streetcar Named Desire*; and the young Karen Allen, a goggle-eyed Laura distraught beyond words over the psycho-metaphoric impact of the broken glass tusk of her tiny unicorn in *The Glass Menagerie*.

The spectators respond with a standing ovation, calling out: "Author! Author!" whereupon the playwright takes a bow.

But for me the real drama happens after the curtain falls.

Again, I tag along with the crowd, this time to the opening night party at the same bar I'd camped out at earlier that afternoon. The booze flows freely, courtesy of the festival producers. And later, with the lights turned down low and the music turned up high, bodies bump, dope is rolled, lit, and passed around. I am thrilled to take a couple of puffs from a joint I estimate to be thrice-removed from the playwright's lips, tapping inspiration practically at the source.

I recognize among the gyrating bodies a gaunt Carrie Nye making cats' eyes at a young James Naughton, while her ever tart-tongued TV-talk-show-host husband, Dick Cavett, sits stoking the playwright's wit. I cannot decipher the question, but the response it sparks is clearly enunciated in that distinctive southern drawl: "I live in a world that's more and more mystifyin' to me, in which my only safe haven is the theater! [...] Damn right, I'm a romantic!"

It's then that I spot the pretty and patient barmaid who served me earlier that day. Emboldened by what I've been drinking and smoking, and by the words of the master, feeling as if they were personally directed at me, I reach out with a brashness that only comes over me in transit and at the theater, with all restraint on temporary hold, and whirl her around to the rhythmic thump of the Stones' "I Can't Get No Satisfaction," taking daring liberties in the dark. She does not resist. We bump and grind up a storm until suddenly she freezes.

—"What's the matter?"

—"He's watching!"

—"Who's watching?"

"My boyfriend," she shrugs, "he owns this place!"

Next thing I know, two heavies have hoisted me up by the armpits, and I'm lying outside on the sidewalk, the brisk breeze blowing down from the Berkshires fanning my hot face. With great effort I manage to raise myself upright and hobble back to my motel, where I drop into bed fully dressed.

But that is only the prelude to my distress.

Primed by all the excitement and the cocktail of intoxicants, my chest metamorphoses into a human jukebox, the RPM beating double-time, sending SOS signals from my heart to my brain and back. I know I ought to call 911, but the effort of reaching for the phone is more than I can muster. And so, I lie there listening to the beat of my heart, hoping I can make it through the night.

Venturing out the next morning, taking deep grateful gulps of air, glad to be alive, I run into a wobbly Mr. Williams, ever dapper in his trademark white linen suit, supported on either side by accommodating handlers, possibly the same gentlemen who showed me the door the night before. Mustering up my gumption, oblivious to their threatening looks, I pull out a pen and timidly hold forth my tattered paperback copy of *The Glass Menagerie* I brought along as a talisman, the play that launched its author into instant stardom. Noticing the ink stain on the writer's callous on my right middle finger, he flashes me a sympathetic smile: "I can see from the ink stain that you belong to the brotherhood of scribes."

Speechless, I nod.

"Tough racket, kid!" he winks, smiles kindly, and with a trembling hand signs the book.

*

Almost exactly a year later, my brother calls to relay the sad news of the playwright's passing, found dead in a New York hotel room, choked on a plastic bottle cap, his system saturated with barbiturates. A wake-up call for me to clean up my act.

*

Cut to October 2019. With two plays produced and five books publishes, I finally make it to the Frankfurt Book Fair on a book tour promoting my most recent book. A little boy, age 10 or 11, rushes into my publisher's booth, where I am signing books, followed by his mother. "Are there any real live writers here?" he asks, breathless. My publisher points to me. "I want to be a writer!" the boy declares. "Is it hard?" he looks me in the eye like he really wants to know.

Dare I reveal all the bumps and bruises, all the disappointments, hurdles and doubts, and the need to develop a tough skin against insult and rejection? I neither want to discourage him nor pump him up with false illusions. He'll have to find it all out for himself. But what should I tell him? I wonder. Which is when Tennessee Williams' sage words suddenly leap to mind. "Tough racket, kid!" I whisper, wink, and sign the book.

V

Far and Wide

Confessions of a Born-Again American Cowboy in France

A funny thing used to happen every time I set foot in Paris. Striding down the dusty tarmac at Orly Airport back in the days of cheap charter flights, the sweat-soaked seat of my jeans clung to my limbs like a second skin, my face felt leather-like, a mask tanned taut by sleep deprivation and in-flight tippling. Jet-lagged joints crackled as my compact five-foot-five-inch frame realigned ligaments and cartilage, converting to metric. I pursed my lips and primed my tongue, preparing to converse with the natives.

And then it hit me, that deliciously unsettling sense of displacement, like I'd stepped out onto the wrong movie set. Everything was strangely elongated and set at an odd tilt and timbre, the caps on the heads of the baggage handlers, the muffled rumble of the bus waiting to take me to the terminal. I scanned the bleak suburban scape, where aircraft roamed like mechanical cattle and factory smokestacks loomed like giant Gauloises cigarettes. The dislocation was complete. I was ready to saddle up. This was my Post-Modern Monument Valley and I was the Marlboro Man sans cigarette.

A curious metamorphosis, I admit, for a short, intro-spective New York Jew of distinctly sedentary habits, whose mount of choice is an ergonomic desk chair, his six-shooter a pc laptop. A guy who rides rough saddle on the IRT and ropes yellow cabs at high noon — I'm more Woody Allen in *Bananas*, for Christ sake, than John Wayne in *Big Jake*! But travel fosters a fluid identity, like the character with interchangeable faces and bodies in the split pages of a children's flip art book.

It all started when I met my French wife-to-be at a New York party. A petite professor of bookish bent and slender figure, she asked me what I liked in life. "Sex, food, literature, and travel," I frankly confessed in drunken French, as I never would have dared do in sober English. In the early days of our experiment in international relations, we would rise at odd hours (a compromise on time zones) and stumble naked to the kitchen wrapped in a single blanket. She craved her nightly dose of chocolate and I my Coca-Cola, though I have since converted to Calvados.

To the folks in her ancestral French Alpine village, my beloved second home for three decades and counting, I am still affectionately referred to as "*l'Américain.*" My first appearance on the scene is the stuff of local legend. Gathering to welcome me way back when, the family were half expecting me to ride up on horseback, when a rented Renault 5 rolled in, a vehicle so small the Duke wouldn't have been able to fold in his knees, let alone fit his ten-gallon hat. This being my first experience at stick shift, I promptly stalled on the village square disrupting a game of boules (a Gallic cousin of bowling). As I swung myself out of the driver's seat, the entire village blinked as one — not unkindly, just a bit bewildered, clearly wondering if I hadn't left half of me behind. Compact Americans seldom made it to the silver screen.

"Get you a little whiskey, you'll be alright!" a guardian angel growled in my ear. Then and there, as if reading the subtitles in my mind, dear Uncle Joubert, since deceased, to whose memory I shall forever be grateful, took me in hand. Popeye's spitting image, this pint-sized, frog-throated, retired seaman from Marseille pulled out a bottle of Johnny Walker and filled his special whiskey glasses to the rim, the kind that when drained dry dissolve the bikini off the bathing beauty at the bottom. "*Eh, Américain!*" He winked and we clinked.

The family took me in with open arms. To these most gracious, country folk, hunters all by avocation, I am automatically linked to their trusty Remingtons and prized Smith and Wessons. Raised on G.I. liberators and John Ford Westerns dubbed in French, they cannot help but superimpose the myth on me, and I am happy to oblige. For whereas, at Paris cocktail parties, I have on occasion been ribbed for tacit complicity in the seemingly unstoppable spread of McDonald's, Disney, and bio-engineering — all my protests notwithstanding — to my adoptive southern French family, I am The Man Who Shot Liberty Valance and helped run the bad guys out of town and give France back to the French.

Am I an imposter? Perhaps. But what a liberating alias it is!

In New York, I am strictly an "indoorsman," all work and no play. In France, I let loose, road horseback, and shot target practice with my late father-in-law. "Ripped it to pieces, the American did!" he boasted to his brothers with a semi-serious grin, holding up the target I'd riddled with holes. And in my heart of hearts, I longed to one day join the men of the clan in their annual wild boar hunt.

The real pay-off came at our outdoor feasts of venison and boar's head prepared, as per ritual, by the hunters themselves, the ribs stewed in a rich civet of blood and wine; the head severed, sliced and simmered, topped with a rich *sauce gribiche* flavored with brains; the tusks passed out as trinkets to the kids. Davy Crockett and Daniel Boone would have felt right at home!

Hardly kosher! you say.

From my mother, whose family ran a poultry stall in the marketplace in pre-War Vienna, I learned how to pick fresh chickens. Contrary to my squeamish contemporaries who purchase their pullets pre-parted and under plastic wrap, I have no qualms dissecting my dinner, cooked or raw, though I do draw the line at buying it live in Chinatown.

French and Americans, we are literally of the same cloth. Let us not forget that the paradigmatic emblem of the American West (and by extension, of contemporary Western Civilization) was stitched together on American soil out of French fabric and Jewish thread. Levi Straus — the peddler, not the anthropologist! — turned a ream of tough material from Nîmes (de Nîmes, hence "denim" for short) into the iconic American garment that would later bear his name.

A born-again American cowboy in France, I have gladly returned the favor. With my French in-laws, we traveled Out West in the States. Together we trekked through the real Monument Valley, the unmistakable setting of every Western worth its whiskey, from *The Searchers* to *Thelma and Louise*, not to mention the popular French cowboy comic strip, *Lucky Luke*. We gazed in awe and wonder at the towering red fingers of rock and, elsewhere, stared breathless at forests of cacti, and true to our shared celluloid dreams, went gaga when we pulled into a roadside saloon to find a serious poker game in progress. On another trip, this one to Texas, we bowed our heads (I, with tear-filled eyes) before the fabled Alamo.

Surely, I'd been training for the part since early childhood, when I wouldn't have been caught dead outdoors without my holsters packed with toy six shooters and a rubber Bowie knife stuffed in my belt for good measure.

But there was a hiatus.

John Wayne, I owe you a posthumous apology! I who shamelessly appropriated your persona as the key to the heart of my Gallic in-laws, betrayed you in life. I was there in the crowd, back in 1974, when you rolled into Harvard Square in an army tank to accept the "Brass Balls Award" of the *Harvard Lampoon.* I did not come to greet you, but to stare at the tarnished symbol of warmongering you represented. They pelted you with snowballs. And though I did not join in the jeers, it was fear, not conviction, that held me back, lest you leap out and throw a punch.

How strange to see the Duke again on TV years later, still scanning the horizon with the same deadpan squint, but with all the feistiness dubbed in French! About to laugh out loud, I wiped a tear from my eye.

Going to France to find yourself is a longstanding American tradition. From Benjamin Franklin to Josephine Baker to Ernest Hemingway to Levi Straus jeans, we've buffed our image on the whetstone of French panache and style.

After 30 plus years of annual hegiras, the exotic edge of France has worn off a bit. I drive stick shift, play boules, drink pastis and swear like a native. A few years back I even accompanied the clan on a wild boar hunt, though our elusive target leapt by in a flash and the only shot I took was with my 35-millimeter lens Minolta, and that one I missed. Still, the thrill lingers.

My French and American personae have evolved a free trade agreement: I let a little Gérard Depardieu into my Woody Allen, with a glass or two of Bordeaux at dinner to lighten up and cut my cholesterol, and keep my John Wayne primed for sunset gallops in the Alps. My venison civet, prepared according to my father-in-law's recipe, makes mouths water in Manhattan. My Texas chili thrills tongues in old Gaul.

John Wayne himself might have been flabbergasted to learn (as I did from my wife, an expert in Nineteenth Century French fiction) that John Ford's classic Western, *Stagecoach*, in which young Wayne made his starring debut, was inspired by "Boule de Suif," a short story by the French writer Guy de Maupassant. Don't tell me the Duke of Monument Valley actually earned his spurs on the Champs Elysées! I can just see his ornery ghost squirm, purse his dry lips and spit out a dubbed "*Ç'est pas pour demain!* That'll be the day!"

Buddha in the Alps

In winter the pink of dusk falls early on the overwhelming whiteness. In spring and summer, the brooks leap with trout and the lush green meadows are dappled with wild flowers. The narrow winding trails of itinerant muleteers, once the only point of entry and egress, were widened into roads in the Sixties to facilitate access to the ski slopes. Crosses mark the junctures between nature, mankind and the ineffable.

Dominating one such promontory above the little town of Saint-Disdier, cupped mid-clap between the slopes of l'Obiou and the craggy cliffs of Le Faraud, in the Dévoluy Massif in the Département des Hautes Alpes in southeastern France, the spire of the 11th-century Chapelle des Gicons, the oldest sanctuary hereabouts, fondly dubbed Mère Église (Mother Church), pokes out of the cliff like a petrified finger.

My late father-in-law was born in a village on the outskirts of Veynes, the nearest city. My wife and I have been making a decidedly secular annual pilgrimage to Saint-Disdier for close to three decades to sample the trout fished altogether un-sportsmanlike — Hemmingway would have been appalled! — from the artificial holding pond in front of the inn at La Neyrette. You can catch your own and have the innkeeper dress your trout nicely *au bleu* or in a *sauce meunière*. The effort of separating the flavorful white flesh from the spine and dispatching it, in a wash of white wine, is sport enough for me.

On my memorable first visit, after lunch over coffee and génépi, the potent liqueur flavored with alpine plants of the genus Artemisia (commonly called wormwood), my wife suggested that the chapel on the hill might make an ideal destination for a digestive stroll.

It was a Wednesday, as luck would have it, the only day of the week on which the sanctuary was open to visitors. We were greeted by the gruff parish priest, who introduced himself as Père Théo. Peering back over his stooped shoulder, his bushy brow echoed the vegetation outdoors and his squinting eyes refracted the few rays of light he allowed to creep in after him through the narrow portal oddly situated at the rear of the chapel.

"*Étroite est la porte, resserré le chemin qui mènent à la vie, et il y en a peu qui les trouvent.*" (Strait is the gate, and narrow is the way which leadeth unto life, and few there be that find it.) He quoted the Gospel with a sly twinkle and a hoarse voice, leading us in after him, his stony expression melding with the wall of the sacred edifice, the wall itself blending in with the pale white cliff out of which it was cut. Dashing on ahead of us, he seemed more mountain sprite than parish priest, the guardian of a hidden treasure.

Time had eaten away at the chapel's inner sanctum, eroding all but a few remaining traces of what must once have been an elaborate series of frescoes, one of the Last Judgment, one of a resuscitated Christ ascendant, and one of Saint Michael dispatching a dragon, its erstwhile fierceness reduced to several stray teeth and a detached tail. "*Venez! Venez!*" Père Théo bid us follow him up a rickety ladder of a scaffolding for a closer glimpse of the fresco on the rear wall.

He flicked on a powerful flash light. A primitive rendering of the Last Supper presented the Savior with bare feet tucked in under his knobby knees at table, his right hand raised, thumb and forefinger curled in something like the sign French chefs and Indian yogis make.

"Look at the way he's seated," I whispered to my wife, "it's the yoga lotus position, for Christ's sake!"

"Shush!" she frowned, a forefinger to her disapproving lips.

But the combination of the Alpine liqueur and the high altitude went to my head. "Père Théo," I called out, "can it be that the Christ is seated in the posture of the Buddha!?"

Silence. Only an American with no sense of world history or geography could come up with such a foolish question.

"Funny you should ask!" he replied after a while, the hint of a smile playing on his lips. "I've heard," he continued, "that the monks who built our chapel and brought Christianity to these parts had previously preached the gospel as missionaries in India."

Good heavens!

A scholar of comparative religion or an art historian would have had heart flutters. Consider the implications. That in the mind of the medieval artist-monk who sketched the sacred scene and the conceptual schema of his ecclesiastical patrons, Heaven melded with Nirvana, the locus of enlightenment, linking the Alps with the Himalayas. That the stiff-fingered V of the conquering Christ Ascendant, a cliché of Byzantine art, bowed to the humble Buddhist curl of thumb and index finger, and that this burst of enlightenment should have been consecrated and recorded in a tiny 11th-century Romanesque chapel in a remote corner of the French Alps and tended by a gruff 20th-century country priest.

Père Théo has since returned to the rock out of which he and his beloved sanctuary were carved.

One winter afternoon years later, after spending the morning snow-shoeing on the nearby plateau of the Col du Festre, I returned on a whim to Saint Disdier to find the sanctuary and its surroundings all cloaked in white. I circled round to the rear, but the chapel door was locked.

But I located his tombstone in the churchyard:

Théophile Eyraud

1926-1999

Curé en Devoluy

De 1969 à 1999

Théophile means "Beloved of God," a fitting name. His spirit still whispers from the beyond in words of welcome (here in my translation) carved into a memorial plaque standing beside the tomb stone:

"If you be Christian or not,
From these parts or just traveling through,
If you be joyous or distressed,
Enter with complete confidence.
This is your house too...
It is here that you will meet
Him who LOVES YOU: GOD."

The stone directly to the right marks the repository of the ashes of a certain René Desmaison (1930-2007), a celebrated French mountaineer, who in the course of his career climbed more than 1,000 mountains, and made the first ascent of more than 1,000 previously unclimbed peaks throughout the Andes, the Alps, and the Himalayas. Desmaison engaged his old friend in posthumous banter recorded in rock (again in my translation):

"Théo, stop
twiddling
your thumbs.
Do something
for me."

And though I don't climb mountains or hold to any prescribed faith, philosophy, or grand design, the memory of those eroded fingers of a Romanesque fresco of the Christ curled and bowed in Buddhist mode intertwined with the image of the twiddling thumbs of that amiable parish priest still move me more than I can tell.

Selfies at the Louvre

Why do people go to museums, I wonder? Is it simply to gaze at and take pleasure in objects of beauty? But beauty is a relative and ever-changing notion. What pleases us today repels us tomorrow. To the contemporary eye, Rubens' plump ladies seem in dire need of a fat farm. If only Ghirlandaio's old man had the benefit of modern advances in plastic surgery to remove the disfiguring warts on his nose! The beams of light that transpose the trace of Christ's stigmata from the sacred son in heaven to the frail limbs of Saint Francis in Giotto's depiction are nothing compared to the lavish laser displays at a contemporary rock concert.

Common wisdom holds that in our communion with the great works of the past we cultivate ourselves, i.e. climb piggy-back on the visions of their makers so as to stretch our own limited vista.

On a nocturnal visit to the Louvre some years ago, I came upon a group of American schoolgirls, along with their teacher and their guide, clustered around the sanctum of sanctums, in a wide semicircle surrounding Leonardo da Vinci's "La Giaconda," or "Mona Lisa," as she is better known in popular parlance, protected by bulletproof Plexiglas and ringed by a guardrail, surely the single most famous and most frequently reproduced painting of all time, the epitome of artistry, much as Einstein's unruly mane epitomizes genius in the popular consciousness.

Much has been made of Leonardo's masterful evocation of Mona's elusive smile, not a full-fledged curl of the lips, but more of a mindful reflection on the idea of mirth, and his depiction of her eyes which his ingenious brushwork accorded an uncanny ability to follow the viewer from every conceivable angle of observation.

I came too late for the guide's erudite explanations. By the time I got there, the girls all had their backs turned to the painting and had whipped out their cell phones, engaged in that 21st-century ritual of shooting a selfie, posing beside their subject, while holding up a high-tech powder mirror at arm's length to meld one's own image with Mona, a modern day "Kilroy was here" to be posted forthwith on Facebook and Twitter and disseminated to the world at large. Far be it from me to pass judgment.

Who's to say that the impression of Leonardo's masterpiece is any less vividly imprinted in their young minds than in mine? Or that they came away from their visit to the Louvre any less cultivated than me? The purist might deem such snapshots as acts of virtual vandalism. But in the wake of an actual dousing with sulfuric acid, a pummeling with a rock and a tea cup, and various and sundry assaults by other warped admirers over the years, La Giaconda is today the best-protected painting in the world. Given the crowds and the necessary precautions, it is in any case impossible to get up close enough to commune with the original. Reproductions are our only recourse.

But culture is a quotient that grows exponentially in the eyes of the beholder. We all have our portable images of Mona engraved in our mind's eye. I'm quite sure the adulation of schoolgirls eager to bask in her reflected beauty would have amused Leonardo no end and given Mona something more substantial to smile about.

The Iron Lady's Measurements

It's 1,665 steps to the top. You don't need to count or climb them. Just to know they're there takes your breath away. Nor does the knowledge that the structure weighs 10,100 tons make you want to try to lift it. But the soaring spectacle of all that stacked metal glimpsed from below and the vertiginous views of Paris from above can turn mere mortals into supermen. The tower lends you its strength and grace, entrancing you each time you visit with a paradoxical impression of massive bulk and airy delicacy, as if its intricate iron filigree had been woven on a giant loom, a gift of the gods.

Mountaintops tend to elicit such awe. The fact that this summit was man-made lends a certain heroism to the mundane. But master builder Gustave Eiffel was not alone. It took a team of 50 engineers, architects, and draftsmen armed with 5,300 sketches, and 250 workers driving in a total of 2.5 million rivets, two years, two months and five days, to complete.

Every seven years, to protect against corrosion, it is painted from head to toe by 25 painters applying 60 tons of paint. "The Iron Lady," as the tower was dubbed soon after completion in 1889, has since changed her complexion six times in accordance with changing tastes. "Venice Red" before being assembled, she was made up in "reddish brown" for opening day, retouched in "brown ochre" three years later, sheathed in five shades of yellow in 1899, re-dabbed "yellow brown" in 1947, "reddish brown" in 1961, and finally in 2010, covered with the bronze-like "Eiffel Tower brown" it wears today to blend with the face of Paris.

It takes 336 projectors and 20,000 light bulbs to light up at night.

Numerous stars have shared its brilliant spotlight over the years, including stage actress Sarah Bernhardt, showman Buffalo Bill, and inventor Thomas Edison, who dropped by during its opening days, the latter bearing a facsimile of his newly invented phonograph as a gift for Mr. Eiffel. During World War I, the tower's radiotelegraphic installation intercepted messages from the enemy, leading to the arrest of the elusive and sultry spy Mata Hari. In 1925, notorious conman Victor Lustig sold it for a bundle to a gullible scrap metal dealer. Two years later, Lindbergh flew over it on his first transatlantic flight from New York to Paris, guided to a safe landing by its glow.

The tower has been parachuted off, dangled from on trapeze, clambered up the outside, bicycled down step by step, and in 1989, the year of its centennial, bestrode by tightrope walker Philippe Petit, of Twin-Towers-fame.

Open seven days a week, 365 days a year, it attracts more than six million visitors each year. The line can be daunting. Is it worth the wait?

An elevator operator I spoke to on my way up from the second level to the summit admitted she'd wearied of the daylight vista, but never tired of the view at night, "rising in a golden glow." And the sommelier at the posh Restaurant Jules Verne on level two, whom I happened to run into on the way down, confessed that "champagne bubbles don't taste any different at high altitude — *mais quand-même!*"

Giddy going all the way down, drinking in the vista, all I could do was grin.

Balzac's Telling Scratches
(and Other Literary Relics)

Much like the relics of a saint, a selection of objects on permanent display at the Maison de Balzac, a jewel of a museum tucked away down a flight of steps in a pocket of time below street level in the posh Sixteenth Arrondissement of Paris, attest to one man's single-minded compulsion to milk his mind and tell the story of his moment.

Among the treasures are a set of writing instruments, including a penknife to sharpen the nib, a gift of Balzac's correspondent-turned lover, and finally, wife, Madame Hańska. Another present of hers, a distinctive cane, graces the same showcase, its turquoise encrusted knob engraved with the coat of arms of his fictional lineage, entwined with a necklace from her childhood. The subject of a book by another admirer, Delphine de Girardin, *La Canne de Monsieur de Balzac*, likewise on display, the cane looks so alive you can practically feel the crush of a sweaty palm on its knob and hear it tap in time to the rhythm of a determined stride on an imagined pavement.

In another room a bronze cast of the novelist's delicate right hand, the knuckles etched with tired wrinkles, ache for a pen.

A place of honor is reserved for Balzac's *cafetière*, a white porcelain coffee cup crowning a matching white pot decorated with blood red bands and the monogram HB, the chalice and cauldron that fueled his 15-hour-long, non-stop writing stints, a regimen that produced some 20-plus books, but strained his heart and ultimately hastened his premature demise.

Here, too, is the sturdy-legged little writing table, the pulpit of his epic sermon on the foibles of the human comedy. Engraved in its walnut surface a cluster of hieroglyphic-like scratches and grooves, a kind of second script, preserve the fluidity of his caffeine-swift strokes. Balzac paid tribute to his table as one might to a long-suffering lover: "Witness of my miseries, my distresses, my great joys, of everything [...] My arms almost wore it down with the weight of my writing."

*

Readers of *The Three Musketeers* and *The Count of Monte Cristo* can slip into the stone narrative of Alexandre Dumas Père's storybook castle, which he dubbed the "Château de Monte-Cristo," preserved as a historic landmark in Port-Marly (Yvelines), just a short RER suburban train ride outside Paris. Designed according to the author's specifications, the house and grounds, including an ornate Moorish-style sitting room and a free-standing neo-Gothic writing studio surrounded by a moat, reflect his rich fantasy and lavish, over-the-top lifestyle. "When you have the honor of bearing the name of Dumas you live the high life [...] and do not refuse yourself any pleasure," he wrote, true to form, squandering the fortune garnered by his prolific pen. The *joie de vivre* of the man is still palpable more than a century after his death in a faded, food-stained menu featuring his favorite concoction, an oyster omelet.

*

The walking stick is balanced, seemingly haphazardly, as if Monsieur Proust had just left it lying where it fell on the polished rim of the brass bed frame following a late-night prowl, before reclining to record his impressions and the maelstrom of memories stirred up by them. The blue bed cover looks freshly slept in. The walls of the cubicle are covered in cork, as was the original bed chamber, to ensure silence. The cork, alas, aggravated the author's asthma. You can practically hear the coughing fits.

The furniture and objects were reassembled for this sacrosanct cubicle in the Musée Carnavelet, in the Third Arrondissement, on the instigation of a friend and admirer, the Countess Anna de Noailles, assembled from the author's final three residences, at 102 Boulevard Haussmann, 8 bis Rue Laurent Pichat, and 44 Rue Hamelin, in the Sixteenth Arrondissement, where Proust finally gave up the ghost.

The collection includes the following objects: an ornate inlaid wooden desk hardly used — Proust wrote in bed —, a bookshelf, a chaise longue for alternative reclining and elbow-propped reading, a carpet, a jade plate, a hand mirror, a monogrammed brush, a tie pin, a silver-plated dish, the aforementioned walking stick, an easy chair, a folding screen, a night table, a lamp, a mirror, various writing utensils, a pocket watch, an agenda, a hair brush, an ebony-handled hat brush, another of rosewood, and an ivory shoehorn — in short, nothing but the bare necessities of a writer's life.

*

As the desk on display in the reconstituted master bedroom at the Maison Hugo, on the Place des Vosges, in the Fourth Arrondissement, reveals, Victor Hugo wrote standing up. It was here that he composed much of his masterpiece, *Les Misérables*, at 1,900 pages one of the longest novels ever written. How did his legs hold up, I cannot help but wonder, in the deluge of all those words and the time it took to put them on paper? Did he never grow tired? I imagine him clinging to the carved oak drawer knob of his desk in the shape of a lion's head, deriving strength from the image of the lion and the fortitude of the solid oak.

*

Paris, the City of Light, has a suburb of darkness. How fitting that I should visit Drancy in search of a faded plaque to a poet's memory on this dark, rainy Sunday, according to the French calendar, the proverbial *Saints de Glace* (Ice Saints Days), as per medieval belief and chronometric prediction, the days dedicated to Saints Mamert, Pancras and Servais, traditionally May 11, 12 and 13, when the saints' names are invoked by farmers to avert the sudden drop in temperature and forestall frost so perilous to prone crops.

The sky turned an ominous dark gray and exploded in a sudden downpour as the bus pulled into town, clearing up and then clouding over and exploding again, unable to make up its moody mind.

The u-shaped, prefabricated complex of the Cité de la Muette, a visionary venture in its planning stage, construction of which began in the 1930s but was never completed, was originally intended to lodge factory workers in a perfectly functional, albeit healthy, environment. But the intended residents never moved in. Plans changed.

The utopian vision devolved a decade later to dystopian ends. From August 1941 thru August 1944, thousands of men, women and children, the poet Max Jacob among them, all of Jewish ancestry, were rounded up by the French police, preempting orders of the Gestapo, and held without adequate food, water, medicine or sanitation in a makeshift internment camp, from whence most were deported to death camps in Poland. Following the liberation of Paris, the Cité was briefly used to intern collaborators, before being cleaned up, cleansed of unsavory associations, and refurbished as a *Habitation à Loyer Modéré* (HLM), a low-income public housing project. Many of its present residents are recent immigrants from North Africa who must surely look with a mingling of puzzlement and annoyance at the visitors who drop by to dig up an unsavory past of which those who live there have no notion.

A plaque at the entrance to Stairway 10 marks the spot where Max Jacob died. Paris is plastered with memorial plaques to poets, artists and composers, but this one tugs particularly hard at the heart strings.

A man of eccentric, often contradictory tendencies, a poet, painter, author, and art critic of Symbolist and Surrealist bent, gay, Jewish, alternately charming and cantankerous, Jacob was among the first friends Picasso made in Paris, and an artistic comrade in arms at the Bateau Lavoir, the legendary Montmartre atelier, lodgings and launching pad of the artistic avant-garde. Following a vision of Christ, he converted to Catholicism and retired to the Benedictine monastery of Saint Benoît-sur-Loire, in Loiret, to commune with God and escape the Nazi occupiers.

His spiritual communion was short-lived. Denounced by a collaborator, he was rounded up and dispatched to Drancy, where he lay, deathly ill with bronchial pneumonia, for which no medicine was available at the camp. Word got out to influential friends along with pleas to try and intercede with the German authorities on his behalf. The artist, writer, and filmmaker Jean Cocteau, who had social connections with high-ranking German military, tried in vain to obtain his release. Rumor has it that, when asked to help, his old pal Picasso is said to have fliply replied: "Max is an angel, he doesn't need my help, he'll grow wings and fly away."

Jacob left no mementos at Drancy. I stood staring at the small metal plaque affixed to the wall in his memory, trying to extract meaning, when a little boy came whizzing toward me on a bicycle so that I was obliged to leap aside, incensed at that moment at what I perceived as the desecration of this solemn place. Why did the French state not designate it as a historic landmark and leave the Cité de la Muette as an uninhabited hollow husk haunted by ghosts?

But then "The Beggar Woman of Naples," a prose poem by Max Jacob sprung to mind. In it the near-sighted poet, known for his trademark monocle pinched between doubting brow and prominent nose, recalls succinctly how he repeatedly dropped alms in the basket of a beggar woman in Naples, surprised at never being thanked, until finally he fathomed upon closer inspection that what he had taken for a thankless mendicant was, in fact, a green wooden crate containing a clump of red dirt and a few half rotten bananas.

At that moment the rain stopped, the cloud cover lifted, and the sun came out. The merciful ice saints interceded. Better, I thought, that Drancy not be a depot of rotting bananas, but a place to learn to ride a bicycle.

Vanishing Vienna

"There was a third man...I didn't see his face."
—Graham Greene

When last I visited Vienna, the natives were busy launching a hot air balloon to combat nuclear arms.

The mood was very lively, very *gemütlich*, very Viennese. Three portly aerialists were to rise in a wicker basket, proclaiming world peace. Actually only one was portly, with a long beard and wild curly locks that took up additional space; his companions, a man and a woman, both blond, trim and elegantly outfitted in a blue and a red jump suit respectively, though colorful, were subsumed by the ballast of his being, fluttering like scarves round his neck.

Trouble was the ton of multi-colored nylon refused to fill. Undaunted by the resistance of the material and cheered on by the crowd, the three took turns climbing out of the basket to blast flames from the mouth of a compact mechanical dragon into the massive bladder on the lawn. And when at last the slumbering giant stirred, a score of sympathizers had to hold it down long enough for the fat man and his friends to clamber back aboard, deliver a few fitting words on disarmament, smash a champagne bottle and soar into the firmament, waving, disappearing through a gap in the clouds.

*

Baroque by temperament, restrained by Catholic creed, Vienna's personality — if a city can be said to have one — is curiously split between a compulsive exhibitionism and an equally powerful bent toward concealment.

Take the proper gentleman I spotted in a pedestrian underpass, peering intently at the ground, peeking up every now and then to meet the eye of a passerby to test the effect of his attire, or lack thereof — his clothing folded neatly in a heap on the bench beside him, he wore nothing but a pair of orange briefs and black nylon hose, but no one seemed to bat a lash. It may well be that people simply didn't see him, that by standing perfectly still, not imposing his presence but silently posing, this latter-day Albrecht Dürer in drag could flash for a selected audience without overstepping the threshold of respectability. In a civic sense, he succeeded in becoming invisible. Or perhaps like President Waldheim, he wore his emperor's new clothes well. The Viennese have a keen sense of propriety combined with a wondrous talent for overlooking extraneous details, a talent that they put to good use some decades ago when sudden disappearances were all the rage.

*

Vienna is a city from which people seem to be forever fleeing.

My father, for instance, did it in the side car of a motorcycle huddling to hide his prominent nose and other suspect features.

My uncle left disguised as a child prodigy due to debut in London pictured in the passport of an accommodating friend.

An aunt of mine married an Egyptian and reenacted Exodus in reverse.

Cousins twice-removed shipped off to Shanghai, Uruguay, New Guinea and other picturesque places.

And my paternal grandfather, a respected engineer who had a hand in the construction or repair — I'm not sure which — of the *Riesenrad*, the colossal ferris wheel (slow spinning insignia of Viennese escapism), and who proudly served his Kaiser as an officer in World War I, left his war medals on prominent display lined up atop his commode with a note: "You know where you can put these!" the day he stripped and swam across the river to Czechoslovakia.

Escape is still a popular pastime in Vienna today.

Consider the conversation I had with an attractive young Viennese native at a cocktail party.

"What do you do?" I asked.

"Oh, nothing really, nothing at all," she smiled a strangely absent smile, "I'm married, you see." Which response would have perfectly sufficed anywhere else, but being Viennese, she felt the need to elaborate. "When I was a child," she said, "my mother took me away on a vacation, I can't remember where. And I liked it so much I decided that that was all I ever wanted to do, to be on a permanent vacation."

Restraint skewed the same tendency in another young woman, turning her escape hatch inwards.

She was seated stiffly erect a few rows in front of me on the No.71 Streetcar to the Central Cemetery, a novice nun in stern black habit without the slightest worldly allure. I was on my way to visit my deceased grandmother, the only member of the family who still maintains a local permanent address. I looked up to check for my stop and a stray hair caught my eye, a chestnut brown strand that broke out of the prison of the young nun's hood fluttering in the wind of a half open window, sparkling in the Sunday morning sunlight. There was something so seductive about that one wild hair dancing about lewdly in contrast to the sobriety of the cloth that I felt a sudden overwhelming desire to see her face.

Eagerly I pushed my way forward through the crowd, convinced that I was about to discover a rare bird whose plumage the common world had never noticed. All else was a blur to me except for that single hair and the mystery it betokened. And when at last I arrived at my destination and turned to look, she turned her face away.

Did she sense that someone was watching her? Did her piety compel her to try to hide?

But the sunlight served me well, and in the streaked reflection in the glass I saw it — Dear God! —: a horseshoe of repressed passion nailed to her brow, clutching in its vice grip any flicker of illicit feeling, any crude diversion from the sacred path.

*

Though I admit I am a mere novice escape artist, hardly a Houdini, still my experience may, nevertheless, shed light on the general phenomenon. Is Vienna's elusive heritage not buried in my heart?

I was standing waiting for a tram at the southeast edge of the Burggarten, on the Ringstrasse (Vienna's grand boulevard), a corner dominated by the seated statue of the poet Goethe exhibiting himself with magisterial disdain, his bronze impassive gaze oblivious to the petty concerns of the slaves of time.

(I had passed him once before, my mind on other matters ostensibly gathering material for a play I was writing, noticing nothing but the pigeons perched on his tarnished head. Thus

I was somewhat surprised, to say the least, to be roused in my sleep by the hotel telephone and to find that it was Goethe on the line, the monument not the man — I'm quite sure of this, since the voice had a hollow metallic tone common to statues and operators and the operator had no cause to call me. The poet introduced himself, said he'd known my mother as a young woman, and might he be of some assistance to her son? — . It was true, my mother had adored him, having taken all his words to heart, many of which she could recall on cue and recite with little prompting; she had carried his collected works with her into exile from Vienna to London to New York.)

Standing face to face with her idol, I smiled at the comedy of dreams, and a curious thing happened.

There was a certain woman I had been avoiding, a painter pushing sixty who clung desperately to the images of her unhappy youth. We had met at her gallery opening: macabre charcoal sketches, shrunken faces with bulging eyes, not very cheery stuff. We got to talking. I reminded her, she said, of a boy she'd known in Budapest before the War who'd disappeared in a transport. Would I, she asked, pose for a pietà in his memory in the buff? Politely, firmly, repelled at the sordid idea, I declined, but the painter kept calling to press me to change my mind until, finally, I changed my number.

I spotted her now on the Ringstrasse advancing toward me from the opera among the matinée mob. She hadn't yet seen me, but the angle of her gaze was set such that it was bound to meet mine in a matter of seconds.

No streetcar in sight, no kiosk to duck behind, no newspaper to cover my face. I wanted to run, but my feet froze beneath me. I wanted to turn my head away, but the muscles in my neck tightened, locking my chin in place.

No way to deflect the inevitable.

And then it happened. The poet came to my rescue by sheer example.

Unable to escape, I had no other recourse but to stand my ground and become a statue. Every joint and muscle in my body stiffened, the blood congealed in my veins and for an instant, the time it took her to pass, I am convinced that my heart stopped beating. And I became an effigy of myself, as still and invisible as a monument, and vanished in contemporary disregard.

*

Other family members found themselves immortalized in like manner. I think of the salt pillars of the Bible, how seeing too much can turn a body to stone.

"What do you think of it?" a woman asked my opinion of the memorial to the victims of the War recently erected on a prominent site just behind the opera. Its centerpiece is a bearded old man on hands and knees obliged to scrub the sidewalk (a posture adopted by my maternal great uncle shortly before his disappearance). "It's a shame!" the woman said, not waiting for my response. "What's done is done," she shook her head, "and such things happened, of course. Put up a monument if you must, but must you put it here? Why not put it someplace else where it's less conspicuous?"

*

Monuments capture the nostalgic spirit of the city. The Viennese have learned to transcend the flux of time by simply standing still and looking backwards.

Stalwart ancients pose in imitation of their beloved emperor Franz Joseph, sporting his famous white mutton chop whiskers.

Indomitable widows permanently occupy streetcar positions clutching their precious poodles in the seat beside them: snarling blinders, bulwarks against age.

Even Viennese punks have something static, ever so faintly fin de siècle about them, as if the leather of their impeccably tattered jackets came from an ancestor's recycled Lederhosen and their safety pin earrings were filched from an aging dowager's pin cushion.

Everyone, young and old, hovers in a somnambulist trance, like photographs escaped from an album.

The effect can be unsettling.

A sleeping beauty perfectly preserved in her century-long repose, Vienna waits for Prince Charming to come and wake her, only the prince is long since dead, the imperial monarchy itself has fallen, the beloved emperor with his mutton chop whiskers replaced by a scowling corporal with a toothbrush mustache and, thereafter, by clean shaven civilians given to selective memory loss, while beauty lies resplendent, a silent movie queen in her outmoded finery, oblivious to time, puckering her lips in anticipation of a kiss.

How rude it would be to wake her!

*

I was just getting settled in a new apartment (a cold water flat in a pre-War building). Having not as yet had any guests, I did not know the sound of my doorbell.

And so it was that I awoke one night in near total darkness to a persistent ringing and reached automatically for my alarm clock. The glowing hour hand pointed to a phosphorescent number 3, but the clock itself was silent. Must be the church bells, I thought, and pressed the pillow over my ears — Vienna has almost as many sanctuaries per square inch as Rome. Then I became aware of a pounding at my door and a muffled command: "*Aufmachen! Polizei!*"

Adrenal terror flooded my veins. I threw off the blanket, jumped into my pants and shuffled barefoot to the door, trembling with historical recall.

"Open up! We know you're home!"

I did as I was told.

My visitors, two faceless men in trench coats did not wait to be invited in.

The one inspected my belongings, the clothes and books I hadn't yet gotten around to unpacking. The other approached my table that doubled as a desk, sat himself down and examined the scattered pages of a work in progress. Then he rolled a sheet of clean white bond into my Olivetti portable and typed as he talked.

"Name?"

"Peter W."

"Nationality?"

"American."

"Occupation?"

"Writer." I shivered, feeling naked without a pen in hand and minus my shirt and shoes.

"Now then, Peter W," he inquired, "where is Peter R.?"

"Don't know," I said, "I just sublet the place from him, I've never met him."

"Where do you send your rent check?"

"To a numbered bank account."

"A curious coincidence, wouldn't you say, that you and he should share the same first name!?"

"A coincidence, yes. Peter is a popular name."

"It seems," said the man at my typewriter, "that Peter R. has disappeared."

A silent pause.

"What are you doing in Vienna, Peter W.?"

"Researching a play."

"What kind of play?"

"An hysterical — uh, historical play."

"Let me give you a word of advice," he said, fingering my manuscript pages.

I listened intently, curling my icy toes. Every writer dreads the verdict of critics.

"Never," he said, "mix fact and fiction!"

I nodded, wondering if anyone will believe that this really happened.

"That will be all," he said, tearing the sheet out of my typewriter, rising from my chair, waving his colleague to the door. "We wish you a pleasant stay in Vienna!"

It was just a mistake, I later learned, an administrative mix-up at the local precinct. Still, word of my nocturnal visitors spread. The widow next door, whom I had often helped with her groceries, refused to talk to me after that. The super and his wife, whom I'd tipped well at Christmas, likewise shunned me. My entrances and exits were henceforth accompanied by a chorus of creaking doors pulled open and slammed shut. My actual departure several months later must have seemed redundant to my neighbors for whom I had in any case long since ceased to exist.

From Vienna with Love
(and Other Mixed Emotions)

Maybe it's the wine, two glasses of crisp white Grüner Veltliner, downed on an empty stomach to still the flutters at the start of my stay. I flew into Vienna a day early and am waiting for my wife Claudie to join me. She's French, and for her Austria is primarily a European neighbor nation steeped, like France, in culture and history, its capital a jewel of a city with grand boulevards, resplendent palaces, world-class museums and concert halls, and cozy cafés. Maybe it's my mood and where I am in life: sixty-four, my parents long gone, and the tingle of time nipping at my heels. Dare I let go and indulge in the city's abundant delights?

A looming anniversary brings the past too close for comfort. On March 12, 2018, it will be eighty years since the *Anschluß*, when German soldiers crossed the border unresisted, jubilant masses mobbed Vienna's sprawling Heldenplatz to welcome the invaders annexing their land with a native Austrian at their helm, and my parents fled for their lives.

That was then, this is now, I try to tell myself, as if Vienna is just another popular destination and I am just another visitor.

*

I'm here on a fellowship from the Österreichische Gesellschaft für Literatur (the Austrian Society for Literature) to translate an impossibly difficult book by the modernist Austrian master, Robert Musil. My English translation a few years back of another book of his, *Posthumous Papers of a Living Author*, is now in its third edition. With my selection and translation of *Telegrams of the Soul*, I helped stoke interest in a forgotten fin-de-siècle Viennese coffeehouse raconteur, Peter Altenberg, who's life-sized, plaster facsimile graces a table at the posh Café Central, his former haunt. But truth be told, translation is a useful emotional front for me, a ploy to prospect raw emotions.

I was touched and torn when, a few years back, on a Central European road trip with her friends, our daughter, Aurélie, eighteen at the time, emailed to tell me how strangely at home she felt in Vienna, where she'd been repeatedly taken for a local. Something about her aura, the faraway look in her eyes, or, as one person put it, like she'd leapt straight out of a Klimt painting.

*

Sifting through a lifetime of keepsakes with my brother and sister in our old family house in Jackson Heights, Queens, shortly before it was sold — a house my brother-in-law, himself the son of refugees, somewhat sardonically still refers to as "Little Vienna" — two tiny, faded, black-and-white snapshots with scalloped edges caught my eye. Mementos of a long-ago Sunday stroll in the Vienna Woods, one features my father in lederhosen bunched up above the ankle; the other captures my mother, a dark-haired beauty in white blouse with puffed, short sleeves, perky peasant skirt and apron. Just a boy and girl out on a date, with no inkling of things to come.

*

My father returned to Vienna on a business trip in 1958. Stirred by the spectacle of his hometown in ruins, still much as it was depicted in the film noir classic *The Third Man*, he reported back with a tug of mixed emotions: loss, longing, nostalgia, and the Schadenfreude of spurned love. His eyes lit up with evident gusto as he described his first bite of a *Heisser*, the original Wiener hot dog, wolfed down at an outdoor stand, so delectable "*daß die Ohren wackelten*" (that "it made [his] ears wiggle" with delight) — one of his oft-repeated Viennese turns of phrase.

Among the souvenirs for my siblings and me was a packet of Mannerschnitten, delicate wafer biscuits layered with hazelnut chocolate cream, the divine taste and distinctive pink packaging unchanged since my father's childhood. Subsequently exported to the States, they remained a favorite family treat until years later, when we learned that Manner had employed slave laborers from concentration camps during the war to manufacture its sweet delights.

*

How vividly I remember our first family trip to the Old Country, in 1962. I was ten, my brother Harold twelve, and my sister Evelyn seven. Pumped up with a feverish pageantry, my ordinarily mild-mannered and parsimonious father splurged and rented a white Mercedes sedan to ferry us back to his erstwhile hometown in style. Making merry at the wheel, with the window rolled down, he crooned a sentimental prewar hit tune: "*Wien, Wien, nur du allein / Sollst stets die Stadt meiner Träume sein*" ("Vienna, Vienna, it's you alone / May you remain forevermore the city of my dreams") — his voice soaked with saccharinity and sarcasm.

On entering Viennese city limits and passing a tram rattling along at a leisurely pace, my mother exclaimed, "*Schaut mal,*

Kinder, die Straßenbahn! Look, children, the streetcar! It's like a living room on wheels!" Tears welled up in her eyes. "The last time I rode it I cried, thinking I will never again see this city I loved so dearly, when, wouldn't you know it, I run into this girl I'd grown up with. Without thinking, I reach out my hand and call to her: "Gerda!" She smiles, her hand shoots out automatically to meet mine, then suddenly she yanks it back and turns away, as if contact with me might be contagious — *ach Ja!*"

My mother's emotions again ran strong at an unexpected meeting in her old neighborhood, the working-class enclave of Rudolfsheim, in the Fifteenth District, with a guy she'd grown up with, now a middle-aged metalworker who ran a basement workshop inherited from his father. At the sight of her, he killed the flame and lifted the lid of his welder's mask, his face drained of color, like he'd seen a ghost, crying out, using my mother's maiden name: "*Jesus, Maria und Josef, die Karpf Mädeln!*" (Jesus, Mary and Joseph, it's the Karpf girls!)

Things came to an emotional head at the monument to the Empress Maria Theresa — Austria's Queen Victoria — the only woman ever to rule the Austrian Empire and by marriage, Duchess of Lorraine, Grand Duchess of Tuscany, and, incidentally, mother of the ill-fated French queen Marie Antoinette. A UNESCO World Heritage site, enthroned on a grassy knoll, sandwiched in between the monumental Kunsthistorisches (Art History) and the Naturhistorisches (Natural History) museums, her imperial majesty's colossal six-meter-tall bronze likeness raised on a granite pedestal, ringed by mounted metal generals, harkens back to a bygone grandeur, to which, despite all, my parents still felt a certain grudging attachment.

But my siblings and I were children, after all. Having spent the morning at the two museums and had more than our fill of culture, we were running around the empress and her entourage to decompress, playing noisy catch in English, when a passing elderly gentleman shook his head in evident disapproval. Decked out in traditional Tyrolean garb, lederhosen, a vest of green Loden material, and a green felt hat with a peacock feather protruding, his cheeks sprouting copious, white, muttonchop whiskers in hairy homage to Emperor Franz-Joseph I, he grumbled in Viennese dialect: "*Eine Schand!* What a scandal! These children have no respect for history!"

Whereupon my mother exploded. "Don't you dare lecture us about history!" she gave him a tongue lashing in Viennese dialect. "These children know more history than you, you addled old fool! Only they don't suffer from selective memory loss!"

The old man blinked twice, as if he could not believe his ears, patted down his whiskers, pulled in his tail, and slunk off, speechless.

We paused in our play, peering from the retreating old codger to the impassive metal empress, to our mother, all of five feet tall, towering in our admiring gaze.

*

"Look, a diabolo!" I shout to my wife Claudie, upon spotting a familiar object in a Viennese toy-store window, a once popular plaything that has recently made a comeback, this one made of two multicolored rubber hemispheres screwed back-to-back on a smooth metal axle, the sight of which immediately transports me back in time.

I remember my mother amazing throngs of spectators,

young and old, in Long Beach, Long Island, where we spent my childhood summers, with a little rubber diabolo my father had brought back from Vienna, first twirling it at lightning speed on a string spanned taut between two sticks, tossing it so high you had to squint to see it against the sun, then miraculously holding up her right stick, beckoning, like Roy Rogers to his trusted horse, Silver, for it to obediently return, land, and slide back down along the axis of the string, upon which, with a smile, she reaccelerated its spin, and again sent it hurling into the heavens. It was the early Sixties, the heyday of the yo-yo and the Hula-Hoop, but the diabolo was a novelty. She taught us how to spin, toss, and catch it, but we were never as good as she.

My mother had been quite an acrobat as a girl between the world wars: turned cartwheels on the sidewalk and boldly leaped from the ten-meter-tall high board at the Schönbrunner Schwimbad, the pool in the summer palace gardens originally built for the exclusive pleasure of commissioned officers in the Kaiser's army. And even in New York, with her feet planted firmly on the ground, she retained through late middle age and well into her senior years a perfect sense of balance, a physical self-assuredness, a confidence of the kind her children have always lacked, as if she'd drained its last reserves.

Yet fear made her twitch whenever the telephone or doorbell rang — a reminder of the ring that presaged her father's sudden arrest. Upon his return the following night he wouldn't tell what he'd been through, just kept trembling and repeating his name with a fierce determination: "I'm still Heinrich Karpf!"

My mother, that erstwhile fearless acrobat and high

diver, never let us climb to the top of the monkey bars at the playground, the Everest of our little world and for me a lifelong metaphor for daring.

*

My wife and I stand waiting for a streetcar, gazing at a political poster left over from the first round of the Austrian presidential elections. As if reading our trepidation — or perhaps he had heard us whispering — a stranger standing behind us clears the air. "Oh no," he says in English, "he's not the Nazi."

"Thanks for the clarification," I reply in German.

Whereupon we get to talking, our exchange following the prescribed sequence of questions every time German syllables roll off my tongue.

"Where are you from?"

"New York."

"How can an American speak German like this?"

"Son of Viennese émigrés, 1938."

"I see." Pause. "Many came from the Ninth District."

"It's where Freud lived, isn't it?"

"Indeed," he nods. "I'd like to show you something, if you will please follow me!"

Claudie and I hesitate. But what else is travel at its best than a willful surrender to happenstance, the geography of chance?

Ernst leads us past Freud's famous address, Berggasse 19, now the site of a museum. It had been raining. Following at a rapid clip, the ozone in the air aggravating my asthma, I ask him to slow down. Along the way we pass a shelter for recent arrivals from Africa and the Middle East. His district, he reports with pride, has taken in the largest number of refugees.

At the corner of Servittengasse and Grünertorgasse, he points down at a clear-topped, square-shaped section of the sidewalk ringed by a metal railing. Raindrops lay like tears on the Plexiglas surface of a small memorial to the Jewish deportees, a memorial that he and his neighbors had a hand in erecting, or rather, digging. Beneath it lie scattered door keys and calling cards with the names of those of who once lived behind the doors and disappeared.

I raise my camera to snap a picture.

"Wait!" he holds up his hand and dashes into a store next door. Rushing back out with a borrowed rag, he climbs over the railing and gets down on his hands and knees to wipe away the lingering drops.

"You know what this reminds me of?" I whisper.

Ernst nods like he can read my mind.

"My grandfather, mother's father, and great uncle were forced to clean the sidewalk."

Just then another man approaches. "Do either of you have any idea how to go about arranging for a *Stolperstein*, a remembrance plaque?" Born in the States, the man explains, he returned as a child with his parents, who themselves had fled on a Kindertransport to England. He now lives with his wife and children just around the block, in the same building from which his grandparents had been deported.

The three of us stare at one another in silence, linked by a dark inkling of a time we did not know, children of the same history.

*

Claudie and I backtrack with our new friend Ernst to visit the Freud Museum. Its holdings are spare: a walking stick, a hat, a few tiny antiquities, a photocopied diploma, facsimiles of awards conferred and later revoked. Mostly copies. Immediately after Freud's departure, the place was ransacked and later used as a temporary holding pen for those less lucky en route to destinations unknown.

"My mother met him twice," I let slip.

"Oh?" Ernst perks up.

"The first time was on the banks of the Danube Canal. She spotted an elegant gentleman with a distinctive chin beard swinging his walking stick, out for a leisurely Sunday stroll with a young woman. A whisper went up in the crowd: 'There goes Dr. Freud with his daughter!' The second time was in London shortly before he died. Already ailing with the jaw cancer that would do him in, he leaned on a cane at Bloomsbury House, where the refugees gathered. *'Habe die Ehre, Herr Dr. Freud!'* (What an honor, Dr. Freud!) she greeted him, one refugee to another. He smiled back, ears tingling with the familiar greeting in a foreign land."

*

Another Austrian friend, Fatima, joins me for breakfast at the Café Domayer, in Hietzing, Vienna's elegant Thirteenth District. A noted scholar of Austrian literature and cinema, Fatima is the New York-born daughter of an Austrian mother and Pakistani immigrant father. She spent all her childhood vacations in Vienna and returns with her children every chance she gets.

My father grew up on the top floor above this very café, a historic locale, in which the "Waltz King" Johann Strauss is said to have fiddled up a storm. Unable to expunge the ever-popular waltz itself, the Nazis squelched persistent rumors of the Strauss family's carefully camouflaged Semitic roots. From the veranda, my father, still a toddler, gazed down one bright sunny day, transfixed by the sight of a procession of knights riding by on horseback, the costumed cast of a silent film in the making.

Fatima and I take a spin around the old neighborhood, to where, on Neue Welt Gasse, a glass plaque marks the site of a synagogue, whose modern Jugendstil design my Grand-father Arnold, father's father, had a hand in selecting from among the submitted architectural blueprints. The short-lived sanctuary, the only freestanding synagogue built in Vienna between the wars, was erected with great fanfare in 1931 and burned to the ground in the organized mayhem of Kristallnacht, on November 9, 1938.

*

Chauvinistically inclined, in the vein of Saul Steinberg's canonical *New Yorker* magazine cover cartoon map, to view my home town on the Hudson as the hub of the universe, I was from an early age infused by my parents with a mingled longing and ambivalence for Vienna as a countervailing vector of sorts, a lost Eden on the Danube. What is a city but a confluence of portable destinies, a great chorus of rapture and dismay, singing and kicking in unison, competing with the phantoms of inherited memory!

Many, myself included, breathed a sigh of relief when, after a faulted first go at it, in the wake of Brexit in Britain and Trump's upset victory in the States, Austria's cliff-hanger presidential elections resulted in a decisive win for Alexander Van der Bellen, the grandfatherly leader of the Greens, the party of inclusion. His opponent, Norbert Hofer, the dapper candidate of the xenophobic far right Austrian Freedom Party, went a goose step too far, brashly pinning a blue cornflower in his lapel, no innocent blossom but the not-so-secret symbol of Pan-Germanic, i.e., erstwhile Nazi, sympathizers. Fortunately, Austrian voters let the blue cornflower wilt on Hofer's lapel.

According to an assessment by the Mercer Quality of Living Survey, cited in February 2016 in London's *Daily Telegraph*, based on a variety of criteria, including housing, safety, transportation, and recreational facilities, Vienna was selected, for the sixth year in a row, as the world's most livable city. History and politics were not deemed relevant factors. Perhaps they're right. Who am I to disagree?

Berchtesgaden — Who Let the Dogs Out?

There is one subject to avoid when visiting the Bavarian mountain resort town of Berchtesgaden, but I didn't know any better. "Which way to Hitler's house, please?" I politely inquired of a big burly bus driver, who promptly turned red in the face and gasped as if I'd just kicked him in the balls.

Perhaps I should explain. I was driving through picture-perfect *Sound of Music* country, from Innsbruck to Salzburg, dazzled by the snow-capped peaks and green valleys of the Austrian Tyrol, mimicking the falsetto refrain of a kitschy yodeling cassette I'd picked up along the way. American-born son of Austrian-Jewish émigrés, my own attachment to this idyllic locale is a complex blend of attraction and revulsion. Faded black and white snapshots in the family photo album capture the youthful glee of my parents on a picnic way back when, mother decked out in a Tyrolian Dirndl tightly cinched at the waist, father in knee-length Lederhosen, before such traditional duds, prized by nostalgic psychopaths, came to symbolize the sentimental trappings of evil. The costume is still popular in these parts.

Distracted by such external stimuli and by the fat Bratwurst doused in mustard and washed down with a mug of beer I had at lunchtime, traveling through my digestive tract, I must have passed the open border crossing unawares. How odd that the German province of Bavaria elbowed its way into Austria when I wasn't looking, looping back in time, reasserting an old bond. The road sign said Berchtesgaden, 15 Kilometers, above an arrow pointing to the right. Certain place names leap out of the landscape like a badly bulging varicose vein. So it was with the erstwhile terrestrial Valhalla and vacation haven of the Third Reich. My steering wheel practically turned itself, drawn by the magnetic force of morbid fascination. All resistance was futile.

Back to the flabbergasted Berchtesgaden bus driver, who promptly leapt into his bus and sped off, passengers glaring needles. A pretzel vendor merely shrugged. A grandmother wheeling a baby carriage pretended not to understand my German. Clearly there was a code word, a way to ascertain directions to the town's key tourist attraction without calling a spade a spade.

"Oh," said the blonde at the tourist office in town, gently rebuking me with a wince and a smirk, "you mean *das Kehlstein-haus*." Relenting, she added with a public relations smile, "You Americans call it the Eagle's Nest. G.I.'s like to visit for the view."

—"*Danke schön, Fräulein.*"

—"Are you a G.I.?"

"Just a Jew," I was tempted to reply, but held my tongue, shook my head, and reiterated thanks.

The game is played with winks and innuendos. I caught on after a while. Flipping through postcard after postcard of breathtaking Alpine splendor at a souvenir stand, wishing-you-were-here takes of hikers in heaven, cliffhangers, cloud bursts and the like, I finally got up the gumption to ask: "Don't you have anything historical?" Whereupon the sales-girl immediately understood and plucked out a secret stash, vintage views of bygone times with SS-Men in black surveying a crowd of tourists.

In the picture they are standing below the "legendary" Hotel zum Türken, now a pilgrimage site of sorts for the nostalgic. The hotel once housed privileged guests of the Reich before being requisitioned by the Gestapo as its southern command post. In the bedrock below, they blasted a vast labyrinth of bomb-proof bunkers. Damaged by the Allies and subsequently rebuilt with its characteristic chalet-style sloping rooftop and wrap-around terrace of yore, today the hotel offers spotless rooms with a view commended by Arthur Frommer. The bunker is now a museum open to the public.

In addition to postcards of long ago, you can also find booklets and videos put out by the local Verlag Anton Plenk with titles like *The Saving of Berchtesgaden* and *The Case of Göring* (as told by the former Nazi commandant), *Phantom Alpine Fortress* (subtitled *Secret Blueprints of the Organization Death's Head*) and *The Obersalzberg at the Center of World Happenings* (including fond reminiscences of good old times by Eva Braun). On a recent internet search, I discovered that the Verlag Anton Plenk promotes these dubious classics in such periodicals as *Der Freiwillige*, organ of the union of family members of the Waffen-SS, and the Neo-Nazi theoretical rag, *Nation und Europa*.

It was not far from here that a wistful Adolf Hitler spent some of his happiest years, from 1926 to 1929, in a simple country cottage, dreaming of world domination, dictating part two of *Mein Kampf* to his faithful acolyte Rudolf Hess, and wooing his half-niece Geli Raubal, who subsequently committed suicide under mysterious circumstances, thereafter replaced in his affections by the photogenic and more durable Eva Braun. Years later, the country cottage was torn down to make room for the Führer's vast *Berghof*.

Nothing but the bunker and the teahouse at the top remain of the formidable compound, which once comprised the barracks for 20,000 troops, five rings of fortifications, and a thirteen-story-high retreat built into an abandoned salt mine, of which only the top story ever saw the light of day. Designed by Hitler himself and built by slave labor, it was here that he welcomed and lorded it over foreign dignitaries, including Austrian Chancellor Kurt von Schuschnigg, who had no choice but to hand over his country in 1938, and British Prime Minister Neville Chamberlain, who, later that year, readily ceded Czechoslovakia, pledging "Peace in our time." Obliterated by the Allies, only the teahouse at the top and the access road to it were spared, and remain a tantalizing tease, a nature lover's perch or a proud reliquary, depending on your perspective.

At 6,017 feet above sea level, *das Kehlsteinhaus* was designed as a site of deep meditation for the Führer and calculated intimidation of foreign dignitaries, with dizzying views of the world according to Adolf. Conceived by Hitler's sycophantic paladin Martin Bormann, it was presented as a gift to the Führer on his 50th birthday, April 20, 1939.

The recorded message on the loudspeaker of the mountain bus, the only mode of traffic permitted on the four-mile-long, single-lane, serpentine road climbing at a 27% incline to just below the summit, focuses mainly on the marvels of engineering, keeping history to a bare minimum. The hairpin curves on the edge of the rocky abyss are enough to preoccupy consciousness, though everybody knows what you're really here for.

A marble-lined tunnel at the bus terminal on top leads deep into the heart of the mountain, from whence a polished brass-lined elevator catapults you up into the clouds.

If nothing else, the engineers of the Master Race certainly mastered stunning views and special effects. Many a cup of tea has surely gone cold in this remote teahouse while the stunned sipper took in the Wagnerian setting. I stepped outside and climbed the bluff, careful to avoid trampling the wild mountain flowers. All around me there was nothing but bare rock and mist and a lone bird of prey circling in the distance. Vertigo apparently kept Hitler from frequent visits. In this I sympathized and stayed well clear of the precipice.

Back down below in a café just off the Visitors Center parking lot, I sipped a tall glass of Bitburger beer (a brand name that rang a bell on account of President Reagan's historic visit in 1985 to the SS cemetery in the nearby town of that name, despite the ardent televised plea of Elie Wiesel not to do so).

The charade finally let down its guard at a toilet stall in the men's room of the mountain bus depot, the most revealing place in Berchtesgaden. Aside from the usual obscenities, etched, inked and spray-painted insignia abounded above a gaggle of *Sieg Heil*'s, with international well wishes in various tongues, including Portuguese and Afrikans. I had to chuckle at a lone Star of David and the Hebrew dictum, "Anachnoo Po!" (We're still here!), which I'd last seen scrawled inside the Arch of Titus in Rome beneath the famous freeze of Israelite slaves in bondage bearing a massive menorah, a spoil of their defeat.

Finally getting my bearings at the end of the day, I made it to the bunker at the Hotel zum Türken just as it was closing.

"Come back tomorrow!" said an unsmiling fleshy Fräulein of indeterminate age.

"Tomorrow, alas," I explained, "I'll be at Mozart's house in Salzburg," and, turning a blind eye to the yellow PHOTOGRAPHIEREN VERBOTEN! sign posted in the window beside selected bestsellers of the Verlag Anton Plenk, I whipped out my camera to update the family photo album.

"*So, jetzt hohl ich den Hund!* Now I bring out the dog!" Brunnhilde snapped, bursting forth with a snarling German shepherd on a long leash — no doubt a descendant of the Hitler's beloved guard dog Blondi — whereupon I leapt clear of its savage snout.

Back at the wheel of the car, I refrained from yodeling all the way back to the Austrian border.

Practically next door is Salzburg, the lovely sentimental kitsch capital of *Sound of Music* country. The code word and cash cow here is Mozart, composer of a concerto or two and excuse for a chocolate confection that bears his image. Mentionable in good company, the Mozart House is easy to find, no subterfuge necessary. Just don't say Haider or Waldheim.

Snapshots and Souvenirs

Oświęcim, Poland, 1975. It is late April, a dark, raw morning that threatens rain. The road winds monotonously through endless gray fields and over an occasional railroad crossing. Our bus stops to let a long freight train pass. Old Frau S. follows the train with her eyes, nodding once for each car. Bemused, she mumbles to no one in particular. "They said to me they said, 'Hey! know where you are?' And I said, 'Nah!' And they said, 'You're in an extermination camp!' And my word of honor, I swear I said, 'What do they exterminate? Fleas?'"

"Is this your first visit to the People's Republic of Poland?" Basha, our official government guide asks.

"Not quite!" Frau M. answers for the others. "Here's a souvenir from my last trip!" — she adds, holding out her left forearm on which a number is tattooed. And she remembers the faces, bald shaven heads peering out through barbed wire — thinking, "Thank God that's not for me!" — and an hour later — "I was bald and naked like the rest, only I was one of the lucky ones." ...And a lifetime later, the first time she returned, she stood paralyzed, gazing in disbelief at the main gate — "So small, is that really it?" — not reading, but mouthing by heart its taunting message: "Work makes you free...work makes you free...work makes you free...I am a free woman!" She laughed; she pressed a hand against her breast and cried. She walked up to the gate and marched right through. No one shouted. No one shot. She did an about-face and marched back again. And back and forth she tore through the open wound, laughing and crying, until her husband pulled her away. And today, thirty years after, she was going back again alone.

Poor blue-eyed Basha is bewildered. She is young and does not know what to make of such strange talk. One tour bus follows the next. Her words are always the same: "We are approaching the town of Oświęcim — Auschwitz, where the Nazi beast built up the greatest factory of death known to man. Though conscious of our tragic past, the Polish people are justly proud of the present. Today, with a population of 40,000, Oświęcim is the site of Poland's largest chemical plant. We will take approximately one hour to tour the grounds of the State Museum."

"Maybe you'll stay one hour," Herr T. breaks in, "but we'll be there all day." Anger took him by surprise. "Excuse me," he smiles sadly, "but we have made arrangements in advance."

*

Two old men approach the main gate. They look up at a line of black metal letters neatly printed against the sky. Straight-backed capital letters, like those with which we filled our first-grade notebooks. They stare a long time as if the meaning were difficult to comprehend:

ARBEIT MACHT FREI

Work makes you free, it says. One man steps back. He has a camera and motions for his friend to pose beneath the gate. The friend smiles and gallantly tips his hat, uncovering a plain black yarmulke. All this happens without a word.

*

Dr. I. escorts us on a tour of the grounds. He is an archivist employed by the State Museum, a sharp, gray, young man who knows his numbers. "In the summer of 1944," he drones in dull monotone, "at maximum capacity they gassed 20,000 a day. Those were the transports from Hungary. And here," he pauses, "Rudolf Höss, the first commandant of Auschwitz, was hanged by the neck by order of the Supreme Polish National Tribunal on April 16, 1947!"

"Such a shame! Why did they kill him?" Frau P. teases with a girlish glimmer in the dark of her eye. "He built this up. I would have let him go on working here with a cage to sleep in at night. And now I would give him a candy. Not spit at him, no! Because spit I have to produce, and I don't work for dogs." She came here as a girl and she went to the left while her friend, who was with child, went the other way. "So I said to a Slovakian girl — We were already inside the camp — I said, 'I'm still waiting for my friend, but maybe with my shaven head she won't recognize me.' I joked, but she didn't laugh. 'For her,' she said, 'you can stop waiting.'"

The ground is dry and dusty. Everywhere wild grass grows like hair. It grows up around the rusted iron rails in Birkenau and in through the cracked cement floor of the crematorium.

"Flowers!" Frau P. shouts with a sudden burst of joy. She skips off into the field and returns with a fistful of dandelions. "No flowers then," she shakes her head. "Children," she warns, "we must be careful not to lose anyone."

*

The women are upset. They do not want to leave me here. They have left too many here already. This is no museum to them. I try to explain about my research, that I am writing a play, that I need to stay just a few days to use the archives and to familiarize myself with the geography of the place. I don't believe a word of it. Nor do they. They look at me with pity and horror. A lost case.

Expressionless now they stare at me through the windows of the bus. They do not wave as the bus departs. Suddenly I am alone and frightened. My first inclination is to run after the bus. I stand there, suitcase in hand, and watch it disappear on down the road. This is a place like any other, I tell myself. I know that I am lying.

*

The silence trembles. I try to listen away. The rain marches like battalions in the night. Sleep will not come. Not yet. I sit up in bed, switch on the light, and run my eyes along the fine, wood-paneled walls. There are three beds next to mine. They are empty. These beds are intended for visiting scholars. I am not a scholar. I am an interloper in this room, stirring up dust and memory here, in the former office of the Commandant. In measured step, Herr Höss paced the polished parquet floor, brooding calmly on the problems of mass extermination. He was a recognized authority. I hear footsteps in the hallway ... boots. I jump out of bed and rush the door. The door is locked and still I am uneasy. The cold floorboards thrill my bare feet. In the window I see myself, a naked Jew.

I look for comfort at the familiar disorder of my clothes, pants and shirt thrown carelessly over the back of a chair, shoes muddy, sprawled out on the floor. But they have a thoughtless thing-life of their own. Things survive, people do not.

*

Under the watchtower, in the gateway through which the human freight trains once coasted to a final stop, a man sells ice cream. His cart is festively done up in bright red and white circus stripes. Children crowd around squealing with delight. He hands out scoops of the cool, white sweetness pressed between two wafers. I am furious. This is no place for ice cream. It has been drizzling all day. Now the rain comes down in thick, heavy drops. I run for cover. The ice cream man makes room. Where is my indignation now? I lick the sweet stuff as it melts between the wafers and wait for the rain to stop. Ice cream tastes good even here.

*

My clothes are wet. There are dry clothes in my suitcase. In the museum there is a stack of suitcases on display, little brown and gray valises, one just like the other. I try to picture what they once contained and the faces of the people who carried them...a foolish game. I will never see their faces. I move on to the next exhibit. But the black letters scrawled on the topmost suitcase catch my eye. I step closer and read the name aloud. "Dora Karpf," I hear myself say. My mother's maiden name! I am running, crying through every room in our house in New York. The rooms are dark. I cannot find her. I know that I have never been born. Then hunger brings me back and I hurry to the canteen for lunch.

*

Now I am walking on a narrow path in the space between two walls of rusty barbed wire. The path is overgrown with weed that no caretaker cuts. It was never meant for walking. A faded black sign with a pale white skull and cross bones cautions that the wire is live. The sign is more than thirty years old. Black birds and sparrows sit between the barbs. Still I am afraid to touch the wire. I think of the old woman's words: "Every day, early — it was still dark, three or four o'clock — we were awakened by the sound of crackling and a scream ... burning flesh ... Jewish suicides."

I circle the Stammlager, the main camp, with its red brick barracks and neatly kept gravel paths. It is Sunday afternoon, family outing day at Auschwitz. Hordes of children roam freely. This is a Polish national monument. I am a Jew, Jew in a cage. I feel strangely at home with barbed wire on both sides. Children point. No one can reach me. This is my past.

Holy Land Blues

Throughout the three-hour-and-fifteen-minute-long flight from Vienna to Tel Aviv, following in Theodor Herzl's tracks, I nursed the illusion of rebirth. It was 1975, and the romance of Zion hadn't yet hardened into a grim reality of tit for tat. Longing to escape from what, in my mythic take of the moment, seemed like the great rubble heap of Europe, to the fragrant orange grove in the desert, I felt giddy with expectation. This sentiment was further reinforced by the comportment of some of my fellow passengers. A curtain separated the plane's rear cabin from the rest, like the women's section in an Orthodox synagogue. I heard muffled whispers and sighs and was dying for a peak, when, at cruising altitude, the curtain was pulled back and the stowaways, Russian-Jewish emigrants hidden for security reasons, let out delirious exclamations of rapture and relief. Processed in the human clearing house Vienna had become in the twilight of the Cold War era, the Russians were on the last leg of their exodus.

I was on an exodus of my own. I'd spent the fall and winter in Vienna researching my parents' severed European roots and the unhappy history that sent them packing. The German woman I was seeing, a former child prodigy, took her cello to bed, which made for an oddly wooden ménage-à-trois, in which I'm afraid the bulky instrument got the best of it. To make matters worse, the police paid me an unannounced visit one morning at 3 AM to investigate my activities, whereupon the neighbors stopped talking to me. The cellist took up with a conductor. And never being able to get my coal oven to work quite right, I slept alone with ear muffs and a ski cap and pecked at my work in progress on an Olivetti portable with fur-lined leather gloves. So much for the chilly charms of Herzl's Vienna.

We experienced some turbulence en route to Tel Aviv, but nothing compared to the hubbub that erupted when, to the rousing background notes of the Israeli national anthem, the captain announced that we were flying over *Eretz Yisrael*. The entire plane, the Russians and myself included, spilled to the right for a heart-thumping, tear-filled first glimpse of the Promised Land. Whereupon the aircraft tipped, and the captain clamored for us to return to our seats, lest our lopsided enthusiasm send the plane into a tail spin. The ensuing panic detracted somewhat from the stirring effect. And though the landing at Lod (now Ben Gurion International) Airport was smooth enough, I nevertheless felt shaken, off-balance, fighting off nausea and foreboding.

*

My Tel Aviv hotel was hardly a Hilton, but the room was airy and the price was right. So what if the door didn't lock and the jammed window rattled at night? A mild sea breeze came as a welcome relief from the lonely chill of a Viennese winter, Israel already being well into a balmy Middle Eastern spring. On my very first night I was awakened in the dark by a distant rumble, and fearing a terrorist attack — an occasional disruption of daily life at the time — I bounded into the hallway. My neighbor's door was ajar and the light was on.

"Was that a bomb?" I cried out with dark misgivings.

"*Vot* bomb?" came the ironic, Central-European-accented reply. "*Sat vas chust* an Arab alarm clock!"

Stepping closer and peering in through the door, it took me a while to locate the speaker amidst the smoke and clutter. The bed was empty. On the floor sat a man of indeterminate age with a sharp face and gray chin beard, a cigarette balanced precariously on his lower lip, and crushed cigarette butts heaped before him, surrounded by open trunks and suitcases, fingering their contents. "I'd ask you in for a cup of tea," he shrugged with what might best be described as a sneer spiked with a smile, "but I'm afraid there's no room and no tea."

"Thanks anyway."

"*Velcome* to *se* Promised Land," he chuckled.

"Loud noises make me jumpy," I excused myself, "I just got here."

"Been in transit all my life," my neighbor fired back with a devil-may-care shrug peppered with pride, "I never bother to unpack. Let the bastards bury my remains in a steamer trunk," he shook his fist at the window, "it's cheaper than a casket."

"Good night," I nodded, though a powder blue dawn was already seeping in through the open window, reeking of seawater, mildew and cats.

*

Hakarmel Market, Tel Aviv. Like an abacus, the bobbing Adam's apple protruding from the long skinny neck of the *Shoichet* (ritual slaughterer) kept count of the kill. Deadpan, he grabbed pullet after pullet by the throat with his left hand, muttered a prayer, and passed a sharp knife quickly across with a rapid thrust of his right, efficiently dishing out death without a wasted gesture, though one of the headless carcasses squirmed on the ground before falling still.

The fruit vendor in the next stall, his face as rough and ruddy as the citrus he sold, sliced and crushed giant Jaffa oranges in a hand-operated press for a thirsty string of customers. It was Friday morning and business was brisk in preparation for the Sabbath. A spilt trickle of orange juice blended in the mud with a steady stream of chicken blood. A stray dog sniffed at this sea of an unsettling shade of red. The fruit vendor kicked the dog. The dog whimpered.

*

Sabbath eve though it was, no milk and honey awaited me. Having neglected to make arrangements in advance for Friday night dinner, I risked going hungry. Rabbinic law, the law of the land in Israel, prohibits any form of transaction involving remuneration construed as work on the consecrated Day of Rest, which, according to Jewish custom, begins at sundown the night before. A couple of restaurants remained open all the same as a concession to hungry tourists and agnostics, but cash was not accepted. The waiter at one such establishment, whose English was even more rudimentary than my Hebrew, pointed from my wristwatch to a bank calendar. It took me a while to catch on to the customary accommodation to the law: I could leave my watch in hock and pay up at sundown, Saturday, when the country reopened for business.

"Can I see the menu, please?"

"Chicken," muttered the man.

My stomach squirmed, a visceral replay of the dancing headless carcass. — "Got any gefilte fish?"

"Chicken," he reiterated.

"Chicken," I nodded, my hunger more pressing than my

disgust.

Patiently I waited, but no food was forthcoming. The waiter just sat there, fingering my watch, looking up every now and then to cast me a quizzical look. Then it dawned on me that I was supposed to fetch my own plate of cold chicken, potatoes and peas that I only now noticed languishing in a halo of flies on the kitchen counter.

The waiter watched me eat.

Toward the end of his short life, dying of TB just outside Vienna, Franz Kafka fantasized spiritual rebirth in Palestine, where he dreamed of opening a little restaurant with his lover, Dora Dymant. She would cook and he would serve, dreamed he — a Sabbath waiter, no doubt, with ample time for reflection.

*

Who can resist the magnetic lure of Jerusalem's Wailing Wall? Every lane and alleyway in the noisy labyrinth of the Old City inevitably leads to this sacred cul de sac, where, on adjoining plots, Solomon erected his temple and Mohammed hiked up to heaven. Moslems flock to the Dome of the Rock, the golden roofed mosque built above to mark the spot where the Prophet ascended to meet his maker. Jews cling to the cramped plateau below, where the lone western wall left of their ruined sanctuary hugs the absence to the east. A wall surrounding nothing. Every Jew reconstructs his own temple from scratch.

The merciful shade of its ancient bricks proved a soothing balm. Religiously unobservant though I be, my head felt light and my legs went wobbly leaning against the symbolic parapet of my people's dispersion. Home at last, I thought. Greatly stirred, despite myself, I shut my tear-filled eyes and tried to meld with the mortar of Zion, and might well have undergone a spiritual conversion, were it not for a tap on the shoulder.

A bearded old man in black hat and long black coat held out a *Talis* (prayer shawl) and a set of *Tephillim* (leather phylacteries), urging me to put them on and pray.

"No thank you," I gently shook my head, figuring he'd understand. "I'd rather mark the moment in my own way." Shutting my eyes again, my silent reverie was stimulated by the eerie, high-pitched, tongue-trilled religious rapture of Sephardic women in their roped-off cordon of female worshipers. I strained to reestablish contact with the sacred rubble heap abandoned, albeit pickled and lovingly preserved in memory for millennia, by my scattered ancestors here on the World's Lower East Side. Can a locale crystallized into a concept and dragged clear across creation re-acquire a physical reality? Surely we've shed enough tears to irrigate the desert, I pondered and sank to my knees, prepared for an epiphany.

But before I could resist, the old man had already flung a prayer shawl over my shoulders and begun to bind the leather thongs like manacles 'round my forehead and knuckles. He rocked and chanted, motioning for me to follow suit. Rising reluctantly, I moved and moaned in the requisite ritual manner to get the old man off my back, biting at the leather like a shackled dog, growling curses under my breath, the spell of sanctity broken.

*

Holiness eluded me at Solomon's doorstep, but I found a glimmer of it in the squint of a sunburned old kibbutznik in an orange grove in the Galilee, where I volunteered to help out with the harvest. "*Mah-ze?* What's this?" he asked by way of a riddle, plucking a grapefruit from an overhanging branch and crushing it in his powerful right fist. Perched on a ladder propped up against a tree he himself had planted in his youth, it might as well have been Jacob's ladder and he a patriarch. Smile lines crisscrossed his wizened face. A narrow-brimmed blue cap pulled down low over his bushy brow blocked out the sun. "That's no juice, my friend," he grinned with fierce pride, "that's my sweat!"

*

Perhaps it was my figurative predisposition primed by all those years of Hebrew School. Something Biblical must have seeped through after all, though the moral was jumbled a bit. Everywhere I turned, parables and riddles hung ripe for the plucking. So, for instance, by some odd climactic fluke, the sunset split down the middle over the muddy waters of the Red Sea, at the Gulf of Aqaba, where Israel and Jordan abut, blushing pink on one side of the border and glowing golden on the other (I can't remember which was which).

*

We'd literally bumped into each other on a crowded bus the day before. She was standing directly in front of me by an open window, a poster girl for Israel in a short, tight fitting khaki-colored skirt, whipping me in the face with her fluttering black mop of hair.

"Sorry," she smiled, making no attempt to tame and bind the savage mane.

"My pleasure," I smiled back, inhaling her scent.

The bus was headed for Nueba, a beach-front oasis of palm trees on the coastal strip of the Sinai in the territory Israel had captured from Egypt in the Six Day War (and has since returned). At the time, Israeli youth flocked there to let it all hang out. Ophrah was going to meet her platoon-mate, Ziporah, and graciously invited me to join them.

A sultry siren of Iraqi-Jewish roots, Ophrah had dark coffee-colored skin and glistening onyx-colored hair, just as I imagine the Queen of Sheba. Her friend Ziporah, of Yemenite extraction, was no less alluring in an Afro that framed her deep brown face like the shade of a palm tree. Heads turned on the beach when the two shed their army uniforms, stripping down to scant bikinis. Is there any sight as sexy as a sunbaked Sabra straining the minuscule triangles of a bikini!

Lining the beach, the male of the species, meanwhile, flexed their biceps and whistled catcalls, disconcerted at the effrontery of a wimpy foreigner consorting with, not one, but two of their nubile fillies. Smiles flashed, winks fluttered, followed by a non-stop volley of lip-smacking come-ons, sassy put-downs and swift repartees. Largely illiterate in Hebrew and hardly Mr. Universe material, I stood on the sidelines and looked on with awe and wonder.

Can this be the same people that languished, pale and anemic, in the dark ghettos of Eastern Europe and cloistered mellahs of the Middle East? What happened to the sallow-skinned, stooped Yeshivah *bochers*, the haggard yellow men who wiled away lifetimes in ill-lit prayer *Stibln*, pining for the metaphysical Sabbath bride to take their hand and lead them to a spiritual union of the soul in an imagined Jerusalem? What happened to the timid maidens and bewigged matrons cloistered behind shutters in Bialystok and velvet curtains in

Fez?

Reborn like brash phoenixes out of the ashes of Auschwitz, having shed all Freudian inhibitions and the baggage of guilt, Herzl's pale brainchildren joined with their tanned Oriental cousins to once and for all times unleash the long sublimated Jewish libido. Once let out, there was no zipping it back up. A little farther up the beach, naturists shed all and dallied in the dunes. Back then Nueba was Eden minus the *don't's*. No skulking deity to chaperone the party. How I longed to go native and join the fun! I'd have gladly given all the book learning I'd amassed for a freewheeling spirit and a competitive physique.

Still, I could not help but notice the effect this unabashed spectacle had on the black-cloaked Bedouin who stood by, bemused, like shadows separated from their own bodies and the land that belonged to them and to which they belonged, eking out a subsistence living peddling trinkets and cold drinks to the interlopers where they had once roamed freely.

"They're lucky we brought culture, Coca-Cola and bikinis, isn't that right, Habibi?" a tour guide quipped in English, pinching the cheek of an unsmiling Bedouin for the benefit of a bus-load of picture-snapping American tourists. The Bedouin did not blink, but I winced.

Were we Jews not wandering desert nomads once, and are we not still Bedouins in business suits and blue jeans, restless dream-driven children of the wind? I thought of my hotel neighbor in Tel Aviv, the man who lived among half-opened suitcases, of all the itinerant peddlers in my restless lineage, and of myself who feel most alive in transit. Was Herzl, the peripatetic prophet of Zionism, not the most compulsive nomad of them all!?

Having imprudently neglected to cover my head until it was too late, I contracted a pounding headache. A Bedouin woman draped in black from whom I bought a cap whispered something in Arabic to Ophrah and Ziporah that made all three of them giggle.

"What did she tell you?" I asked Ophrah.

A proud smile lit up the beautiful Sabra's mahogany features. — "She said, 'Black is beautiful!'"

The darkness and the absence of posted street names in Ophrah's Eilat neighborhood and my deficient Hebrew made it difficult to pinpoint the address she'd scribbled on the inside flap of a book of matches soaked in sea water. I rushed about the barracks-like blocks of prefabricated apartment complexes, pleading with every passerby, unable to follow the rapid succession of "*yamins*" and "*sminas*," left and right gesticulations.

Needless to say, I arrived more than an hour late. The coffee was cold. So was Ophrah's welcome. The photograph of a soldier boyfriend, whose existence she had failed to mention (but who, she suddenly let slip, was due back from active duty later that evening) hung on the wall beside an army-issue Uzi.

"So tell me, Ophrah," I asked, feeling flustered, frustrated, ill at ease, far more meta than physical, "what does it mean to you to be Jewish?"

"There's my yardstick," she gestured with a proud grin at the firearm on the wall. "This is my land," she stamped her shapely sandaled foot, raising a cloud of red clay-colored dust. "That's the border," she pointed a finger out the window toward Aqaba, whose lights flickered in the distance, the condensation of a golden sunset. "Anybody crosses under my watch, I measure their grave in the cross-hairs."

*

Back in Tel Aviv I fell ill, addled by the same ball of fire that the Egyptian Pharaoh Akhenaten recognized as the supreme deity, that swirling bundle of gases that kindled a loquacious shrub, etched the headlines into rock and led a stuttering tour guide with a lousy sense of direction and his complaining entourage on an extended budget sightseeing tour of the Sinai — hotels and meals not included — I fathomed too late why Moslems and Jews cover their heads.

Feverish and semi-delirious with sun stroke, not wanting to return to my seedy Tel Aviv dive, I accepted the gracious invitation of paternal cousins thrice-removed to convalesce at their apartment in a posh suburb.

On Friday nights, Daniel, a senior official with the Israeli State Department, sucked hot tea through a sugar cube, Russian-style, and strummed on a guitar, regaling friends and family with deep baritone renditions of Yiddish folk songs from his youth. The tender melodies and sentimental lyrics clashed with his grim account of survival in the forests of the Ukraine. A large and powerful man, Daniel had little patience for the unhappy past except as a preamble to the present.

But come Sunday morning, as I languished on the terrace and tossed on a couch in the living room, Daniel's wife, Liuba, a still handsome woman in her late fifties, paused on my prompting from her housework to reflect on the fragments of a shattered Old World left behind. She told me of the day she came home to her Warsaw apartment house, forewarned in the lobby by a well-intentioned neighbor not to mount the steps to the apartment where her father had swallowed the cyanide capsule he kept close at hand in anticipation of his imminent arrest. Of going into hiding with forged Aryan identification papers. Of working as a nurse in a German military hospital, and looking out one day to see the Ghetto in flames and burning women and children leaping out of windows. Of squelching her tears, lest she reveal too much, while the Poles pointed and laughed. She told me of the handsome young Nazi surgeon who one day out of the blue declared his love, proposing marriage, whereupon she fled in the night, never to return.

To the remembered ruins of Solomon's fallen temple, Liuba added the rubble of her own incinerated Polish youth. I never asked, though I was sorely tempted, if, given the hostility of neighbors on all sides, Israel did not sometimes feel like a gilded ghetto. Soothed by her chicken soup, vaccinated by her sadness, I soon recouped my strength and recommenced my exodus.

*

In Jaffa, I sat in an Arab café, sipping Turkish coffee, smoking an occasional cigarette for conversation's sake, while gnawing at green olives big as fists.

*

In the northern hill town of Safed, from whence, the true believers say, the Messiah will one day emerge, I too was dazzled by the ethereal blue light that sparked the wild reverie of the Kabbalists, though this time I made sure to wear a hat.

*

In nearby Meron, I hiked up to the cave of Hillel, the

ancient sage known for countless wise dicta, including his
most famous: "If I am not for myself, then who will be for
me? And if I am only for myself, then what am I? And if not
now, when?" The story is told of a skeptic who once sought
out Hillel's spiritual nemesis, the humorless Shamai, and
challenged him to tell all there was to learn about Judaism
while standing on one foot. Annoyed, Shamai chased him
away with a stick. Then the skeptic challenged Hillel. And the
latter replied: "Do not do unto others as you would not have
them do unto you. That is the essence, the rest is commentary,
now go and learn." While bowing my head to Hillel's memory,
I hopped about on one foot in homage to the skeptic.

*

On a hilltop in Haifa, I sat cross-legged on a low stone
parapet, peering down through the lush verdure of a public
park, flirting with the blue eyes of the Mediterranean,
reflecting on my hybrid Semitic and Teutonic roots trans-
planted in Anglo-Saxon soil stolen from the Manhattan
Indians. What else are we Jews, wherever we may wander,
but displaced Mediterraneans? But something distracted my
eye. It took me a while to fathom that the fuzzy pink patch
in the clearing was no cluster of desert fruit, but a latter-
day Adam and Eve actively engaged in the pursuit of knowledge. The leaves both framed and camouflaged this Holy
Land peepshow, upon which I gazed with a thoroughly unholy
thrill, from which I was roused by a high-pitched cough from
the throat of a white-bearded gnome, round and red as a
medicine ball, who walked up and declared out of the blue:
"From the cross *off se* young gentleman's legs, if I may make so
bold, I can tell he is looking for a *vife*. The knees cry out your
need. Permit me to introduce myself." Whereupon this Jewish

232   EPIPHANY OF A MIDDLE-AGED PILGRIM

Santa Claus plucked out a wrinkled, tea-stained business card, one side of which was inscribed in Hebrew, the other in English, S.J. Friedlich, Matrimonial. "I *haf* a long list of available brides, all of good family," he pandered, practically salivating, so eager was he to drum up business.

"I'll think about it, thanks," I said, somewhat taken aback, indeed stunned — had he not caught me with my pants down, so to speak, and bared the loneliness of my loins? About to pocket the card, I might well have called him the next day or the day thereafter had he not plucked the card back out of my grasp.

"If not now, when?" he shamelessly plagiarized Hillel, replaced the card (no doubt the sole facsimile) in his vest pocket and walked off in a muttering huff, probably scaring off Adam and Eve, for when I looked back the clearing was clear.

*

The fresh water springs falling from the cliffs of the Judean Desert over the oasis of Ein Gedi on the western shore of the Dead Sea might just as well have been a mirage. This is the lowest populated place on earth and surely one of the hottest. A dip in the Dead Sea hardly helps. The bather emerges un-refreshed, his body coated with oil slick and salt brine like a fugitive sardine escaped from a can. Parched and unforgiving though the surrounding desert is, humanity has been seeking out this fertile nook to refresh the spirit at least as far back as the fourth millennium BC, as an unearthed sacrificial altar of a Chalcolithic temple attests. In caves nearby, John the Baptist's ascetic brethren, the locust-eating Essenes, fled civilization such as it was to submit to the elements and scratch their impressions on papyrus scrolls. Jesus could have strolled the oil slick of the Dead Sea without a spill, had he not perfected his act on the Sea of Galilee.

At the time of my visit, the youth hostel at Ein Gedi lacked most creature comforts — no cold drinks, no air-conditioning. A lone ceiling fan in the lobby scattered flies and spread the heat thick as honey. Come nightfall, sleepless guests and staff spilled outdoors to mingle, soaking up a dark illusion of coolness.

It was here that I witnessed and participated in a sacrificial rite. Among the female lodgers, a German blonde, big-boned and a bit ungainly, though not unattractive, was surrounded every night by a swarm of admirers, employees of the hostel. She worked in the kitchen, I think. Taunts and teases with insinuating undertones were carelessly hurled and awkwardly rebuffed. Neither party appeared to know the other's tongue.

What began as seemingly playful flirting intensified little by little into something more serious. Like a storm cloud, the circle of lust shifted about from the brightly lit hostel entrance to an unlit corner of the patio, where paws grabbed and were slapped back. But just as things threatened to get out of control, the seemingly passive object of everyone's lust turned the tables on her aggressors, making clear with the flick of an imperious index finger that she — not they — was pulling the strings. With growls and groans of protest and a flutter of arms, those not chosen scattered like whimpering dogs in search of another bone.

"Why don't you try your luck?" Yossi, a dish washer who slept in the bunk above mine, egged me on one night, as the circle dilated and contracted and I found myself sucked from its periphery ever closer to the center of attraction.

"She's not my type," I shrugged, unaware that the German woman and I were standing back to back.

Whereupon she whirled about. Her impudent gaze took me in and spat me out. — "*Warum nicht? Vy* not?" she shook off the implied rebuke. "*Komm, Liebchen!*" she commanded and I followed. Accompanied by a chorus of catcalls, we strode out into the Biblical Wilderness of Ein Geddi, where David hid out from the wrath of Saul and John the Baptist cleansed his soul through self-denial, in the pursuit of knowledge.

*

Though I flew back to Vienna shortly thereafter to bid farewell to the cellist and retrieve my Olivetti portable and other belongings left behind, my visit to Israel actually wrapped itself up a year later at a Syrian belly dancing club on the South Side of Chicago. The show had already started as I tiptoed past the tables and elbowed my way through the crowd to a narrow strip between two white-tiled pillars reserved for standing room. The sagging ceiling, the dense cloud of cigarette smoke, the press of bodies around me and the remoteness of the exit door all served to multiply the claustrophobic feel of the place. As the dancer's hand cymbals clashed and the mustachioed oud player plucked and strummed his instrument, I tried to keep my cool.

Like every other member of the mostly male audience, my eyes were riveted to the ripple and roll and the dancer's rhythmically gyrating hips. It would be a lie to suggest that licensed exhibitionism and leering are not an essential part of the experience, but at its best, when performed by a lithe and supple dancer swaying in sync with the oud's mournful wail, the belly dance tames the libido, elevating the spectator's lust to an art form, just a twitch short of ejaculation.

At the end of the first dance, I followed the lead of the man to my immediate right, stuffing dollar bills into the elastic band of the dancer's skirt as she brushed by for tribute. Not stuffed in with proper aplomb, my greenbacks fluttered and fell like Autumn leaves. Red in the face, I had to stoop to pick them up and replace them.

"First time?" my dollar-dipping mentor inquired, the ash growing out to a precarious inch on the unfiltered Camel dangling from his lips. "My brother's a bit shaky too, eh Säid," he grinned, motioning with the tip of his cigarette at the unsmiling man to my left, the latter as lean as the former was fat.

Säid said nothing, he just stared.

"Säid doesn't talk much," his brother explained, "ever since he stepped out of an Israeli jail. One year of solitary confinement in a cell the size of broom closet."

I didn't ask what he'd done.

"Where are you from, my friend?" asked the garrulous one.

"New York," I coughed, the cigarette smoke aggravating my asthma and malaise.

"Jewish?" He practically spat out the question, the ash of his cigarette tumbling in an avalanche.

I nodded.

"Better leave now!" he advised, as silent Säid clenched his teeth.

*

In Israel, meanwhile, the flaming sword of the cherubim stationed east of Eden has been replaced by tanks and suicide bombers wrestling for the deed to the tree of life. A new wall has gone up to buttress the weeping stones of the old one — and all around the earth opens her mouth to receive Abel's blood. Rebirth is on hold for the foreseeable future.

The Art of the Deal

The day my wife and I arrived in Marrakesh, the thermometer topped 105 degrees Fahrenheit in the shade, we unwittingly paid three times the going rate for a cab from the airport to our hotel, we rented a rattletrap at what we naively thought was a discount, and proceeded to have two flats on purportedly "brand new" tires. Assailed by hordes of adolescent would-be guides, we were at a total loss until a canny stranger stepped out of the crowd, informed the kids that we already had a guide and chased them away. Mustafa, with whom we were now "affiliated," like livestock to a shepherd, led us back to our hotel where we resolved to leave the country immediately. Fortunately, we slept on that decision.

It hit me suddenly the following day at the tanner's stall in the souk, the outdoor market where Mustafa had taken us "just to please our eyes." Pointing to a cream-colored camel's leather footstool at which we'd glanced with vague interest, the tanner scribbled a figure in the upper left corner of a checkered pad and handed it to me. The price was outrageously high. One moment I was livid at being taken for a fool, the next moment a light went on in the convoluted Casbah of my brain. I scribbled a ridiculously low figure in the bottom right corner. The tanner scowled. "Look," I said, pointing to my wife, "that's my queen! I'm the king. Now let's sit down and play chess!" His scowl immediately inverted into a smile. I'd understood that it was all a game. We passed the pad back and forth, and I came away a half hour later, camel's leather footstool in hand, with the tanner's grudging admiration for a match well played.

Most Americans accustomed to shopping mall mores find bargaining an embarrassment, something seedy that your great aunt Sadi or uncle Silvester did while squeezing the fruit or feeling the material. We expect our commodities cellophane-wrapped, our meat and produce sticker-priced, and seldom say more to the person who sells it than please, thanks or charge it.

But in Morocco, as in much of the rest of the world, bargaining is a way of life. You bargain over everything from marriage dowries to speeding tickets. The taxis have no meters, but passenger and driver have mouths. And though car rental agencies, native and international, list their rates in orderly columns in glossy brochures, just like back in the States, the actual price you end up paying fluctuates with each transaction. Practiced with a varying degree of expertise by every Moroccan man, woman and child, bargaining tests the mettle, sounds your character, pits will against will and wile against wile, and also, incidentally, can be a lot of fun.

The uninitiated tourist has two choices: he can look on and let himself be milked, or learn the rules of the game and join in, responding with the same blend of blarney, charm, cunning, savvy, and seduction.

"Hello, Ali Baba!" the tailor from Tangier, the goldsmith from Fez, the tanner from Marrakesh all greeted us with glistening teeth and a golden grin. "Come look! Just to satisfy the eyes!" And before we can even think of straying to the competition, octopus arms are sweeping us in. The decor is authentic Oriental, the scenario seldom varies.

"Be seated, my friend!" our host always insisted, pulling

out a pair of low, wobbly stools or stuffed leather cushions. Steaming glasses of mint tea appeared on knee-high round metal tables. Smiles abounded and sincere words of welcome ricocheted against false teeth. What followed was pure burlesque, vintage entertainment, if taken with the right attitude. Depending on the nature of his ware, the proprietor pulled out a genuine "antique" dagger and tested its tempered blade on a hair plucked from his assistant's pate; or spread an ornately patterned rug at our feet and swore (with a carnival grin) you could fly it all the way home and never get airsick.

Take my tangle with the tailor from Tangier as a case in point. "Such a lovely lady!" he complimented my wife, coaxing her to try on a pair of *"pantalons climatisés"* (air-conditioned harem pants), span a necklace round her neck, and slip a pair of gold embroidered slippers on her "alabaster" feet. Then once again complimenting the beauty of *"la gazelle"* with renewed enthusiasm, he turned to *"le gazeau,"* the befuddled buck, and sprung an astronomical price. But I was ready.

Custom demanded he ask at least three times what he hoped to get (more in the case of Americans, known for their gullibility and cash flow). No Moroccan would ever take such a first quote seriously, but tourists are always worth a try.

I replied with the proper response: a brow raised in stunned disbelief, signifying in silent pantomime: You gotta be kidding!

The tailor gallantly deferred to my objections with an obsequious palm. It was my turn now to present a counter-offer, contrapuntally as preposterously low as his was high, a tenth of what I might agree to pay. Pretending disinterest, I remarked that though the garments in question were indeed attractive — never offend the merchant or his merchandise outright! — I'd seen their equal elsewhere for less.

True to his prescribed role, the tailor wrung his hands and swore I was out to ruin him, to drive his innocent children out begging in the street. And furthermore, "Monsieur surely cannot recognize quality when he sees it! Feel this leather — genuine camel! Touch this cloth — 100% silk! Surely Monsieur is jesting, but to prove that I too have a sense of humor," he laughed, rapidly regaining his lapsed composure, "I will give you this fabulous garment, hand sewn and embroidered by the King's own personal tailor, for the price of a pair of jeans!" (Note: Levis cost a king's ransom in the Third World!)

Since he now had come down a feather, I too had to give a hair. And so, the bargaining continued, offer vs. counter-offer, until my wife and I had sipped our last drop of tea, no refills forthcoming, and I detected a flutter of impatience on the tailor's lips.

This was the moment of truth, or rather, the moment immediately preceding the moment of truth, an essential distinction every poker player will recognize as the bluff that ups the ante.

"Very well, my friend," the tailor grasped my hand in feigned defeat. "You play a hard bargain, Monsieur, but I will let you have the whole lot, necklace, dress, and slippers for 1,000 Dirhams!"

"Sorry," I shook my head, sighed politely, grasped the hand of my "gazelle," and made for the door. "I can give you 500 Dirhams and not a Dirham more, or else I won't have the money left for dinner!"

The tailor, of course, refused, and as we exited his premises, we cast our sights on the stall next door, waiting for one of two things to happen. Muttering curses under his breath, he would either let us go (an unlikely eventuality), or drag us back in. For now, and only now, like a luscious date begging to be plucked from the sagging palm, the deal was ripe.

Transaction completed, the tailor and I shook hands. Something more than goods and money were exchanged: an acknowledgment of mutual respect, the satisfaction of a game well played, with the implicit possibility of a re-match, Allah-willing, tomorrow or another day.

Impressions of Senegal

The bus headlights graze windows and walls, scattered car wrecks, flashes of light; a faded, red, fifteen-foot Marlboro Man with forehead missing adds an incongruous note — the way familiar images get jumbled with the strange in dreams. Earlier, at Yundum Airport, on the far side of the customs fence, a band of little boys wove through the moves and jerky gestures of a break dance, minus the music. It is 3 AM Gambian time. The air is heavy and hot, though not as heavy and not as hot as I had envisioned. When we climbed out of the plane, for an instant I feared opening my mouth, lest I inhale swarms of imaginary insects. Relieved, though somewhat disappointed at the apparent lack of fabulous flying things, I take my first exploratory gulp. Some people worry about the water when they travel. I worry about the air. Asthma. Bad attack in Paris last night before leaving.

*

6 AM, Novotel, Banjul, Gambia — Africa explodes suddenly at daybreak, almost a cliché of itself, in the myriad chirping and trilling of a thousand birds. Hotel breakfast of pineapple, cornflakes, toast and tea — residue of British colonial rule.

*

There are twelve of us on the minibus to Ziguinchor, in southern Senegal, including the driver and a guide, both Senegalese. The engine is purring impatiently; we are waiting to leave. At the last minute, two hulking sunburned Frenchmen climb in, one tall and blond, the other short and stout, with a thick black beard and a fat cigar spitting smoke. And while the guide is busy on the roof of the bus, securing the newcomers' luggage, Adonis grabs his seat.

"That's the guide's seat!" Claudie protests, incensed at the behavior of her compatriots.

"Is that so, sweetheart!" the cigar-smoker jeers.

The blond chimes in, "You can shove your guide back in with the luggage!'

Both erupt in raucous laughter.

"Racists!" cries Claudie, a petite spitfire of Paris '68 persuasion.

Adonis is stunned. "Oh no, not at all!" he insists, half grinning it off, half wincing at the sting of the word. "We love the people and the country," he explains. "We have a house in the village and come here every year."

Later, the guide, a young man slight of build, climbs in; the blond shoves over in his seat, pulls the guide down beside him and throws an arm affectionately around the African's shoulder. He offers him a cigarette and soon the two are joking and laughing like old friends.

"I'm sorry," Claudie apologizes at the first rest stop.

"Not at all" — the Frenchman smiles good-naturedly and shrugs his shoulder. "You see, we understand them very well," he says, beaming with paternal benevolence at the guide. "It's they who are the racists, not us," the Frenchman jokes.

The Senegalese cracks a cautious smile.

"They won't let us come too close," Adonis sighs, turning around to exchange a wink with his bearded companion, whose cigar hangs limp between his lips, gathering ash as his hairy chin bounces to the rhythm of the bus.

*

My wife's watch (our only functioning timepiece) has stopped, and it is just as well. Time is hardly a matter of hours and minutes here, but a succession of cloudbursts punctuated by spells of bright sunshine: summer is the rainy season. The bus proceeds through the various Gambian and Senegalese military and customs checkpoints with a minimum of bureaucratic flak. The deeper we drive into Senegal, the greener it gets. This is the Casamance, the fertile breadbasket — or rather, rice basket — of the country. The Trans-Gambian Highway, a rare paved thoroughfare just recently completed, winds through the wide vistas of flooded rice fields, dotted with tiny figures knee-deep in the mud wielding wooden furrows that look like oars. It cuts through forests of sleek, long-necked palms; towering silk-cotton trees alive with storks and pelicans; and squat baobabs, with their thick gray trunks and knobby, tusk-like branches, looking more like sleeping elephants than trees; and the oddest of all, the red clay projections that interrupt the green consistency of nature like phallic fingers or some obscure prehistoric constructions — termite hills, monuments to the subterranean intentions of an ancient race of builders.

*

Ziguinchor, Senegal — "The first cock crows at 5 AM, the second at 6," our friends Michael and Marika, both anthropologists doing fieldwork here, inform us; they are our bridge to this world. Other things to remember: Step on the mud where it's green or you'll slip, but don't confuse weed with rice

— it wouldn't do to trample the sprouts of your neighbor's crop. I am up early, seated alone on a flat stone on the porch of our house. The air is alive with the clink and crackle of breakfast fires, water splash, bird trill, early morning human chatter and the ever-insistent cock crow. I have heat rash on both arms and am still suffering from asthma, and yet at this moment none of that matters. There are too many other impressions, more vivid, more insistent. People smile with friendly curiosity as they walk by on their way to the rice fields. Two little pigs appear in the yard, followed by a flock of inquisitive baby chicks. The neighbor's boy comes by to watch me write. He stares at the motion of the pen on the page, studying the strange black scratches.

*

The streets run "three-way" in downtown Ziguinchor: one way for the vehicles — motor scooters, bicycles and tin-can taxis; one way for the foot traffic; and one way for the chickens, cows, pigs, goats and mules. Things can get congested, what with an ornery old goat and a honking taxi angrily contesting the right of way. Still, somehow, by Allah's will, everything keeps moving. Where we live, a little way out of town (past the orphanage and the French lycée, past the bridge where government soldiers with loaded machine guns aimed at the road effectively replace traffic lights), in the district of Koloban, there are no streets. Squatters' huts, thatched or tin-roofed (for the upwardly mobile), are clustered around a maze of footpaths. You find your way by signs and signals: the large pigpen, the green-walled house, the rain-ravaged ruin, the chant and chatter of little boys in the yard of the Koranic school. And in any case, as the Mandingo say: He who has a mouth can never get lost. For everyone knows everyone in Koloban, and even the stranger is soon included. From a Western standpoint, things are backward here: no electricity, no telephones, no plumbing, no running water, no murder, no burglary, no muggings, no rape. At night, in the pitch-black unilluminated darkness, you may risk wet feet, a tumble in the mud, or the wrath of a swarm of hungry mosquitoes, but sitting around a kerosene lamp or stumbling home, you feel a sense of safety, a comfort in the proximity of other people, a feeling of belonging as if at last you have found your corner of the universe.

"*Eu-errara!*" (Good evening!) Idrissa, the master tailor, greets us as we approach his family fire.

He is a tall, lean man of consequence, justly proud of having trained and turned out eight apprentices in the art of needle and thread. His smile is open and the welcome in his voice is sincere. There has been some confusion, it seems, for although our friend Michael had understood that we were to come for dinner tonight, we may well have been invited for yesterday or the day after tomorrow. No matter. Now we are guests and guests must eat. The beef is stringy and tough, real animal muscle. The tailor tears it apart with his agile fingers and drops a few strands in each corner of the collective rice bowl. Later, back at our host Ernest's house, a second dinner of chicken in peanut sauce, a local specialty, is waiting. We cannot refuse; guests must eat.

*

There is no sound as piercing as the desperate squeal of a pig that knows it is about to die. It is the Feast of the Virgin. On this day the Christians, still an influential minority in a predominantly Moslem country, kill pigs. In a little less than two weeks, on Tabaski, the Moslems will kill sheep. Christian and Moslem are neighbors; so are sheep and pig. We run back behind the house, following the trail of the animal cry. Four men are holding down a medium-sized pig with its hind legs secured. Pigs are strong.

Ernest, the *responsible*, or headman of the district, studies the animal's pulsing throat. He is a short, fine-featured man of indeterminate age, with a tired, time-worn expression. His words and gestures are decisive and deliberate, nothing wasted. "Pigs and goats shriek at their slaughter, sheep don't make a sound," he explains, passing the knife several times quickly across the animal's throat. The pig's shrill shrieks cut like blades of sound through the hot and silent air.

"How do the other pigs react to the death of one of their own?" Michael, the anthropologist, asks.

Ernest laughs. "Just like us," he says. "Death is the same for us all."

The pig lies writhing and sucking for air as its blood spurts through the incision. It takes a good ten minutes for the animal's throat and belly to stop twitching. Meanwhile the men have gathered, drawing invisible lines with their eyes, pointing out their portions of the still-living flesh. In America we buy our meat neatly wrapped in cellophane; surely those round, red, antiseptic slices never came from a thing that cried and kicked. At last the twitching stops and the shriek fades to a thin gurgle and goes silent. Now pans of boiling water are brought to singe and soften the bristle and hide. A Gillette razor does the job nicely. Chickens and roosters amble on over to sip the blood on the ground. Even a few little pigs escaped from a nearby pen stroll by and sniff with interest. The carcass is now being divided. Ernest has claimed the ribs, a choice cut, for our dinner.

*

The same green frogs that frightened and revolted me when I first dropped the bucket into the family well to get my bath water are now a comforting, cheerful sight, a comic relief in the morning ritual. In separate little round booths surrounded by a screen of rice straw and bamboo, we wash and take care of our bodily needs.

Still dripping from my sponge bath, I step out from behind the screen to find a young woman staring at me. Wearing a brightly colored *paigne* (a wraparound robe) and a man's red woolen cap, with a toy whistle strung around her neck, she looks like a clown or a lunatic. Her eyes intent upon me, she puts the whistle to her lips and blows a loud, shrill note. I stand there shivering, embarrassed and more than a little apprehensive, as Ernest's wife, Virginie, and other women, old and young, gather round. Virginie, a slender, stately, regal-looking woman of late middle age starts clapping and singing; the others follow. Now the young woman with the whistle leaps into the air and stamps her feet, dancing wildly to the rhythm of the clapping hands, grinning in crazed delight. An old woman chants a song, which must be either funny or obscene, because everyone, including the mad dancer, is laughing. The dancer leaps higher and comes down harder, swirling and stamping faster and faster, more and more furiously, until she collapses onto a stool, panting and gasping for air.

Realizing my puzzlement, Virginie explains. This young woman is in the charge of a local women's society. She came here from a village in Guinea Bissau, where she repeatedly lost baby after baby in childbirth. Finally, she had a healthy baby that lived. In gratitude for this, she changed her name, moved to a strange place and consecrated her life to the service of the women's society, prepared on certain occasions to act the fool and do whatever they wish. Her husband may visit, but she must stay here, for it is the women now, not her husband, who are bound to take care of her. "This is our custom," Virginie concludes, punctuating her words with indecipherable smiles and a raspy kindly laugh.

*

"Toubab! Toubab!" (Whitey! Whitey!) The little children squeal with delight and run up to us as we bicycle by, fighting forward for the chance to graze an arm or a hand with their tiny trembling palms, to touch that strange fuzzy colorless skin. I am reminded of an essay by James Baldwin in which he recounts, during a period of time spent in a little village in Switzerland, how all the children would run up to touch him whenever he passed, never before having seen black skin. It is part game, part children's ritual, a mixture of "chicken" and "tag." Go ahead, touch the Toubab, I dare you! They seem to be cheering, challenging each other on. No malice is intended; we take no offense. Whether it brings good luck or protection from evil or just a prickly thrill, no toddler would forgo the chance. We are four Toubabs — four chances to touch the unknown.

*

Three girls are waiting for us on the road to Babadinka, just outside the village, where the rains washed the bridge away. Yesterday we left word that we were coming — left word, quite literally: a message scrawled on a rumpled piece of paper handed to an old man seated at the fork of the road, with instructions to hand it on to the first traveler bound for Babadinka, who would, in turn, take the message to Michael and Marika's friend Landing — "Special delivery!" It is dusk now –the girls sent by Landing to meet us have been waiting since morning, not knowing when to expect us. Days are different here: like an endlessly elastic rubber band, they stretch until suddenly the light has reached its limit and miraculously then you find yourself at the door of your destination as the darkness snaps in behind.

*

Landing's house is round and big, the biggest in the village. He designed and built it himself. Landing is a young man of formidable character, a man of ideas, a leader. There is no fat on his short, muscular torso, and his bright smile belies a subtle spirit.

"Three blacks and three whites all want to cross a river..." He holds forth with a chuckle, launching into a favorite riddle. "They have but one dugout between them and the dugout can take only two at a time, but if the whites should outnumber the blacks at any moment, they would eat them. So how," he asks, eyeing us with an ironic twinkle, "can the blacks get safely across?" The solution isn't simple. It takes us all evening to figure it out, using three black beans and three white grains of rice to help visualize the problem.

*

Working in the rice fields is no joke. I have never gotten wetter, muddier, thirstier or more tired in my life, and I will never again be able to swallow a mouthful of converted rice without gagging — Minute Rice indeed! Landing takes us into the marshes and shows us how to fling a fisherman's net, and together we wade out to the *Ile des Oiseaux*, where at sunset the branches of the trees are all aflutter — white, black, yellow, red and blue, with song. For dinner we feast on the little carp we caught, over rice, and as usual the mosquitoes feast on us.

*

7 AM, Hotel Aubert, Ziguinchor — Claudie's watch is working again. This note so as not to forget the overwhelming rush of relief at once again having a room with a bed and sheets and a light bulb overhead and a sit-down toilet and a hot shower and screen windows and, wonder of wonders, an air conditioner. In this cool, conditioned air, behind the anonymity of a numbered door, we lie a thousand light-years away from the world outside. I feel some longing, yes, and some guilt toward the people we have met who have been so kind to us, and who could not in their wildest dreams imagine themselves in such a room. I stare at Claudie's bare legs where she has kicked the sheet away. She comes to slowly; our smiles and bodies meet: we do not have to worry about mosquitoes. There is a pool in the courtyard under the palm trees, reserved for the guests of the hotel. I run out in my underwear, oblivious of propriety, past breakfasting Europeans, and dive. Swallowed by the filtered kiss of the water, I know that I have left Africa behind.

Détente at the Russian Baths

Wading into the murky pond in the Russian village of Roshchina, about a two-hour train ride from St. Petersburg on the Gulf of Finland, I initially mistook the decomposing mass floating at knee level for a dead fish and only later noticed the drainage pipe. Environmental protection had not been a pressing Soviet priority.

Feeling soiled, unsettled in mind and body, I welcomed the recommendation of our Russian friend Margarita, at whose old wooden dacha we were staying, to visit the local *banya*. It was Saturday afternoon and we were not the only ones with bars of soap, rough sponges, and leafy *veniks* (trusses of dried birch branches) in hand, heading for the baths.

The once whitewashed façade of the local facility was in dire need of a fresh coat of paint. The bathhouse itself was shoebox-shaped, 1950s nondescript, but there was something cave-like and primeval about the faded blue, paint chipped interior, as if humans had been coming in out of the cold for a ritual cleansing ever since the first amphibian crawled ashore.

The ancient Scythians did it, according to Herodotus. So did omnipotent czars, wealthy boyars, impoverished peasants, conspiring revolutionaries, pious priests, and party apparatchiks, and so to this day does every Russian man, woman and child, at least once a week. A predilection for the baths transcends any question of personal hygiene and social class, but, I suspect, even in summer, is an antidote to the lingering chill of the long hard winter, a bearlike need to hibernate, and as such deeply rooted in the Russian soul. And though the once excellent Soviet medical system has fallen into disarray since Perestroika, the baths, commonly known as "the people's first doctor," remain a cherished remedy for every meta- and physical malaise, with vodka a close second.

An ardent devotee, Margarita, a woman of late middle age — the walls of whose cramped apartment in St. Petersburg are hung with drying bushels of birch — insists the baths "will cure whatever you've got," citing its multiple restorative virtues for the circulation, respiration, fortification of the immune system and hormonal balance, and adding, with a wink at my somewhat reticent wife that it likewise enhances matrimonial bliss.

To tell the truth, I too had sudden misgivings when Margarita led my wife through a door to the left and I shuffled alone past the ageless, expressionless matron armed with a mop standing guard at the entrance to the men's section, shed and deposited my clothes on a wooden bench in the changing room, and stood up stark naked, acutely aware of my circumcised penis, the only one in the crowd — all the more so when the mop-wielding matron ambled by — though the blank looks of my fellow bathers registered no response. Americans mask embarrassment with a smile. Russian faces are unvarnished, gruff as unpeeled potatoes.

My sense of malaise grew as I passed from the changing room, via the urinals, into the washroom — the matron following with her mop — where naked men dumped buckets of frigid water over their heads. Having come this far, I told myself there was no retreating now. I did like everyone else, doused myself with a gasp and a shudder and dodged through a heavy wooden door into a burning inferno. The blast of intense heat literally took my breath away. Suffocating and feeling like the skin would peel off my bare feet — nobody had warned me to wear slippers — I staggered to one of the surrounding bleacher-like benches, on which I deposited my body for roasting. Only now did I dare look up.

I had entered what appeared to be a den of hooded sadomasochists gathered in a circle round a heap of red-hot stones, their faces glowing, sweat dripping, gleefully beating each other with birch switches, preparing, so it seemed, to engage in human sacrifice. What folly brought me here? There was still time to cut and run, I pondered in a wild panic, incapacitated by the heat that burnt the hairs in my nostrils, when a man pushing sixty-five or so tapped me on the shoulder and nodded for me to bend over. The first sting of the birch switch on my back smarted. I didn't feel much after that.

Beckoning for me to follow him back out into the washroom, he filled a bucket with melt-off from the Polar icecap, and dumped it over my head. (I would have welcomed a little global warming just then.)

"*Harasho!* Good!" he grunted, having pegged me right off for a foreigner.

The tooth-rattling shock of the first bucketful was followed by a flurry of not altogether disagreeable tremors at the second and third, as if the inside and the outside, ego and superego, resolve and resistance, met and melded at the transom of the skin, the dead epidermal layer of which he scraped off with energetic sponging.

"*Spasiba!* Thanks!" I sputtered one of my three words of Russian through blue trembling lips.

And back he led, and I followed from the ice box into the furnace, where the heat hit with a colossal wallop, sucking the sweat out of my every pore, practically ripping off my very envelope of self. But now the tenderized birch leaves left to soak in a bucket of hot water had softened into a balm which he pressed against my chest, wrenching open every bronchiole and alveoli, jump-starting respiration.

Several buckets of ice water and several bakings later, I followed my new friend back to the changing room, feeling giddy and light as a hot air balloon.

"Alexey!" "Peter!" we introduced ourselves.

"*Gdzie*? Where from?" I gathered the gist of the question from his facial expression and hand gesturing.

I hesitated, wondering, as I often have while traveling in recent years, if I ought not pretend to hail from someplace anodyne like Andorra. Warsaw had recently agreed to let Washington plant a missile shield on Polish soil. It was 2008 and hostilities were simmering between Georgia, an American ally in the post-Cold War era, and the break-away Russian-speaking enclave of Abkhazia, pitting Tbilisi against Moscow on the brink of war. The U.S. was pushing for Georgia's inclusion in NATO. Tensions between Washington and Moscow were once again on the boil.

"American," I muttered, half hoping he wouldn't hear me.

"American!?" he repeated in disbelief.

I nodded, awaiting the worst.

Whereupon a smile erupted on his lips, the first I'd seen in Russia, and rippled, as word spread, like a wave of welcome across the faces of my fellow bathers, thawing any lingering icicles of distrust.

Our conversation was elemental, replete with more good

will than comprehension. We made do with my three words of Russian, some French, a pinch of German, and a sprinkling of technical English supplied by a young engineer named Nikolai who'd worked in Ireland, diluted and washed down with sweet gulps from a shared bottle of kvass, the traditional Russian equivalent of Coca-Cola.

"How you find Russian bath?"

"Hot."

This elicited a peel of laughter.

"And Russian women?"

"Krasotka," I employed a term Margarita had taught me, roughly translatable as "hot number," to describe the blond bombshells parading nightly on the Nevsky Prospect, St. Petersburg's fashionable amalgam of Fifth Avenue and the Champs Elysées.

More laughter.

"What you do?"

I mimed fingers striking a keyboard.

My fellow bathers looked baffled, the engineer ruling out mechanic, masseuse, and pianist, in turn, till a flat-faced man with Mongolian features, a grinning Genghis Khan, piped up: "Hemingway?"

"Dostoyevsky, Gogol," I grinned back.

Brows were raised, eyes opened wide and heads nodded with a respect and admiration no American locker room crowd would ever have mustered for my craft.

Then and there I suddenly had a vision of a new kind of détente. Why not henceforth hold all high-level diplomatic talks in the banya! Have ambassadors, foreign ministers, and heads of state strip naked and face off, sweating out their differences and beating out any lingering post-Cold War gripes with hot wet birch switches. It's a climate far more conducive to compromise than that of the committee room. And though the Russians may, admittedly, have an unfair advantage, being better able to withstand the heat, subsequent talks could always be held on the beach in Hawaii. Just a thought.

Waiting for my wife and Margarita, as agreed, in the bar next door, I sat purging my entrails with vodka and salt pickles.

One by one, my friends filed in for a spiritual lift, though we did not initially recognize each other dressed in the dimly lit room.

"Hemingway!" Genghis greeted.

In the doorway leaned the expressionless matron minus the mop, silent witness to our ablutions, she who kept the floor clean and the rocks hot from morning till night, high priestess of the Russian baths, whose gaze belied nothing of the midriff bulge and other failings of aging manhood.

"*Krasotka!*" I winked.

Even she cracked a smile.

And we all clinked: "*Nasdrovya!*"

The Catalan Lottery Ticket

It is February, 1974, a year before the dictator Generalissimo Franco's demise. Things are still tense in Barcelona. The angst may be a bit less overt here than elsewhere in Spain, muffled by Catalan defiance and big city swagger, but evident all the same in the wary gaze of the locals. At night, the wind howls like hungry dogs. The dogs howl too. Their skinny profiles hug doorways, creeping in and out of alleyways, casting wary shadows.

The one-legged night clerk in my no-frills pension, presumably a veteran of the civil war, who sits, watching soap operas on a black and white TV set turned up so loud I wonder if his hearing might not likewise be impaired, insists, much as I try to dissuade him, on personally escorting me to my room, limping ahead, key in hand, whether out of kindness, duty or distrust, it is impossible to determine.

My bed is a virtual suspension bridge, the metal frame sagging low, the ribs of its grid protruding through the thin mattress, creaking and rattling every time I flip over from back to belly, and belly to back, in a futile attempt to get comfortable. The walls rumble whenever anybody above or below flushes the toilet. I try to find a pattern in the silent pauses between flushes.

I am serenaded, meanwhile, in my restless stirring by the blind lottery salesman stationed late into the night on the street corner directly below my window, whose toad-like indecipherable croak: "Pari! Pari!" he has trained to soar several decibels above the sound of traffic. I prop myself up on my right elbow, peer out the window, and watch him straining his neck in all directions like a submarine periscope, as if by a vestigial reflex mimicking the motions of sight. And while I never saw him sell a single ticket, I wonder with the idle logic engendered by lack of sleep, how, if he ever sold one, he would know if he was paid the right amount and manage to return the correct change? Wrapped in multiple layers of clothing and a ratty blanket, I try to assume a semblance of comfort, and finally catch a couple of winks in between flushes and croaks.

Having dutifully done the tourist thing in the preceding days, admired Gaudi's unabashedly quixotic architectural take on faith in the Church of the Sagrada Familia, Picasso's grim depiction of maternity and other somber, quasi-realistic tableaux of his blue funk period on display at the museum that bears his name, and tried in vain to get the parrots to repeat "fuck a duck" at the bird market on Las Ramblas, I decide to seek spiritual serenity.

So I set out late the following morning by train and bus to visit an ancient monastery some 40 miles northwest of the city, where the raging current of the Llobregat River carved out the jagged white peaks of the Montserrat (literally serrated mountain), and where mankind somehow managed to insert itself into the ravines of an inhospitable cluster of natural skyscrapers, leaving traces that date back to Neolithic times. The Hermits of Santa Maria savored its solitude in the 9th century. They were followed, in turn, by the Benedictines, who sandwiched the Basilica of the Monastery of Santa Maria de Montserrat into a snug pocket of conglomerate gray rock to house La Moreneta, Our Lady of Montserrat, a black wooden Madonna and child. The sculpture was fashioned, legend has it, by the Apostle Luke, and discovered by shepherds attracted by a bright light and heavenly music emanating from a nearby cave where it had allegedly remained safely hidden under Moorish rule.

The mother's hands and the child's feet have been rubbed to an eerie nocturnal finish by the kiss and clasp of the devout. (No real live black mother and child would be treated with such reverence in today's anti-immigrant climate.) The basilica fills daily with busloads of the hobbling and the heartsick and droves of giddy schoolchildren dying to lay their hands on the exposed fingers and toes and rub off as much good luck as they can get. La Moreneta's touch is said to engender miracles.

Irritable from lack of sleep, I cannot bear the noisy little worshippers jostling with the cripples to rub off a finger- or toe-hold of Lady Luck.

To escape the throng, I hop the funicular up to the Santa Cova, the cave in which the Madonna was allegedly discovered, but it too is mobbed, so I hike on upwards, oblivious to time and altitude. The Malo Valley looms far below, and only a few crows disturb the perfect peace. Weary after a while, soothed by the silence, I sit down and am promptly overcome by sleep.

When I awaken, the sun hangs low above the craggy hood of Sant Jeroni, the tallest of the peaks. It gives me pause to see the darkness closing in and to fathom that I am all alone on a mountain top, so I hurry back to the funicular station.

Hopping with holy hikers just a few hours before, the place is now deserted, the windows all shuttered. Outside the door a mule stands tied to a railing, swishing its tail back and forth to shoo away flies. I call out, but there is no answer. The mule and I exchange doleful looks. I tiptoe past him and knock at the door. No response. I pound at it with clenched fists and press an ear against the wood to listen within.

My efforts finally pay off. The door swings open, accompanied by a volley of incomprehensible curses, and out steps an unsmiling man with a thick black mustache, cradling a shotgun. His eyes are red, his breath reeks of wine. He is not pleased to see me. My Spanish being rudimentary, and Catalan nonexistent, it takes my tongue some time to shape meaningful utterances, patching together a hodgepodge of rudimentary Spanish, chin tilts and lower lip inversions. — "*Por favor, signor, que hora*–please Sir, what time the next funicular down–*abajo?*"

"*Mañana!* Tomorrow!" he grunts back.

I think for certain he must have misunderstood and so I repeat the question, emphasizing the word "*abajo*," pointing downwards with a shaky right index finger.

"*Mañana!*" he repeats, his patience increasingly frayed.

"*Fu-ni-cu-lar?*" I take pains to enunciate each syllable, plucking out and waving my return ticket.

"*Cerrado!* Closed!" comes the definitive reply.

"*Como abajo?* How down?" I sum up my distress, trying to fashion a convincing smile with my anguished cheek muscles and twitching lips.

"*Allí!*" There!" he says, pointing with the barrel of his shotgun to a sign nailed to a tree indicating a trail, and promptly slams the door shut in my face.

Obliged to ponder my precarious situation, I run through

possible scenarios. What if I stumble and sprain an ankle? What if I lose my way? What if I run into a wild animal, a wolf or a bear? What if I am accosted by a bandit or a member of the dreaded Guardia Civil? Anything can happen, I tell myself, whipping up my fear.

The mule and I exchange doleful looks again. I have no choice but to knock again.

Finally reappearing, the man with the mustache is tipsier than before, casting nervous glances at my jacket pocket, out of which pokes the handle of a foldable umbrella, still a novelty at the time, which, I only realize in retrospect, he must in the fading light and in his drunken stupor have mistaken for the hilt of a handgun.

"*Por favor!*" I repeat, raising my eyebrows and shoulders in dismay, flashing my return ticket.

"*Caminas!* Walk!" he snarls back, and again shuts the door in my face.

So I saunter past the mule to the signpost, and follow the trail until it divides into a fork, one prong of which leads into the dark woods and the other dips at a precipitous angle down a steep ravine, with no indication of which direction will lead me to salvation.

The sun is setting. Dismayed at my limited options, of either falling to my doom or having to spend a cold night alone in the woods on the mountaintop, I panic, do an about-face, and return to the funicular station. Pressing my ear to the door, the only sound I hear is the racing thump of my own heart. I knock, and since there is no answer, pound wildly.

The man with the black mustache, who does eventually reemerge with the shotgun now raised to eye level, is clearly disinclined to patience.

Drawing a diagram with a stick in the dirt, I desperately try to explain that there is a fork in the trail, and plead with him to show me the way.

Walking on ahead, with the shotgun cocked and pointed at the small of my back, feeling like a disposable character in a Spaghetti Western, I am convinced that at any minute his drunken right finger will twitch and tug at the trigger. I direct silent prayers at the Black Madonna. Though a Jewish agnostic, true to my traveler's credo I always entrust my destiny to the good will of local spirits, figuring her maternal instinct will kick in.

When I come to a halt at the fork in the path, he gives me a nudge with the gun barrel in the direction of the woods. Terrified, I start running without turning around, figuring it is better to risk getting lost in the woods than to land a bullet in the back.

I stumble all the way down and make it just in time to catch the last bus from the basilica back to the train station. The bus is almost full. Climbing aboard, exhausted from running, panting for breath, I scour the vehicle to find the only empty seat beside — you guessed it — the man with the black mustache, who greets me with a grin and passes me his wineskin pouch.

My prayers to the Black Madonna, an equal opportunity dispenser of mercy, paid off. That night I sleep soundly, oblivious to slouching bed frame and flushing walls.

After checking out the following morning, I buy a lottery ticket by way of offering.

*

Cut to the present. In a heap of papers, inveterate packrat that I am, I discover two snippets folded together, a return funicular ticket and a wrinkled receipt, the digits faded but the memory intact, a souvenir of Barcelona. For all I know it was a winning number.

Epiphany of a Middle-Aged Pilgrim in Tea-Stained Pajamas

"In every way, then, such prisoners would recognize as reality nothing but the shadows of those artificial objects."

—Plato, *The Republic*

Convalescing from recent illness, comfortably ensconced in a black leather easy chair, I sit perfectly still, the paper spread open on my lap, careful not to spill the steaming contents of the tea cup resting on the crook of my knee or stain my fingers on the ink of distant unrest. Sickness seals you in that way with a callous disregard for the world beyond your four walls. Unmoved by the big news of the day: the usual potpourri of war, famine, and scandal, I am about to nod off with a long, drawn-out yawn when a minor news item catches my eye, an article concerning the whereabouts of a missing painting by the 17th-century Italian master of dramatic effect, Caravaggio, an artist I once adored. And suddenly, altogether unexpectedly, a caption identifying a black and white photograph of the painting in question as a Nativity stolen from a church in Sicily in 1969 strikes like a bolt of chiaroscuro lightning, disturbing my tender balance, splattering me with tea and memory.

At middle age, revelation is a messy business.

According to the report, Marino Manaia, a Mafia snitch and self-styled authority on stolen art, the State's key witness at the corruption trial of former Italian Prime Minister Giulio Andreotti, then in its second year, broke the monotony of the interminable legal proceedings with the revelation that it was he who, 27 years before, snatched the "Nativity with Saints Francesco and Lorenzo" from the Church of San Lorenzo in Palermo — snatched it right out from under my eyes, altering, if ever so obliquely, the course of my life!

Cut to Italy, Summer of '69. A 17-year-old aesthete, I am on a quest to track down every Caravaggio canvas from Florence to Palermo. Having interned in my senior year of high school at The Metropolitan Museum of Art and briefly flirted with the idea of becoming an art historian, my compulsion looks strictly legit to my parents, who are relieved that my raging hormones should find such a salutary "cultural" outlet.

The truth, of course, has little to do with culture as such. I am stirred by the filthy feet of Caravaggio's virgins and the jarring blend of tenderness and violence in every brush stroke. Other artists make you stand in awe before their handiwork, Caravaggio sucks you in. At the Uffizi in Florence, Isaac squirming under Abraham's knife mirrors my own malaise ("So when are you gonna get a haircut already!") and Medusa somehow reminds me of my mother. At the Galleria Borghese in Rome, I try David's destiny on for size, clutching Goliath's head in his hand, trembling with the knowledge that but for a well-aimed pebble, Goliath would have been clutching his.

The New Testament tableaux move me too. Six years of Hebrew School training notwithstanding, I am morbidly fixated on martyrdoms. And in the Church of Pio Monte della Misericordia in Naples, amidst the angel flutterings of "Le Sette Opere di Misericordia," I leer at a young woman brazenly baring her breast for an old man to suck while a nobleman's lackey strips the clothes off a corpse.

Which brings me to Palermo in search of a tame Nativity, having run out of crucifixions and beheadings.

It is 4 PM or thereabouts and this sprawling ancient slum is devoid of its hibernating hordes. The only soul in sight, a dead ringer for a balding apostle, with leathery skin and a loose-lipped smile, assures me he can show me the way for a few hundred lire. Having shaken me down for the price of a drink, he leads me to the wrong church and leaves me with a shrug: "*Mi dispiace, signore!* They must have changed the street signs."

By this time Palermo is squirming with life. And though every man could have modeled for Matthew, Peter, or Paul, every woman for the Madonna, every child for an angel or Christ, nobody seems to know where the church is. These are the same streets Caravaggio traipsed between commissions, duels, and vendettas, I tell myself to assuage my mounting frustration. When, finally, I do stumble on the battered façade of San Lorenzo, its heavy metal portal is locked and I collapse like a beggar on the steps, cursing Caravaggio for ever having ventured south of Rome, before I notice a cat slipping in through a side door.

"Where is the 'Nativity' please?" I ask an old man slumped over on a bench inside, who may or may not be the sacristan.

"*Nella capella!* In the chapel!" he points to a parcel of darkness to my left.

Twice I circle the church, peaking into every sacrosanct alcove, nook and cranny, but there is no sign of it.

"The Nativity!" I insist, gently shaking the old man, who has since drifted off to sleep.

He looks up with a scowl and limply points in the same direction.

"Show me, please! *Per piacere!*" I gesture, holding out a 1,000-lire note, which magically awakens his interest.

The sacristan perks up. We take the same direction he previously indicated, stopping before a chapel recessed in a curl in the wall. "*Ecco li, signore!* Here it is!" he points, crossing himself.

"*Dove?* Where?" I scour the vacant wall.

The old man strikes a match. Grumbling unintelligibly, he shoves me to the altar, atop which a small black and white photograph hangs askew crudely affixed with strips of yellowing tape to the bare wall. It is, I realize on closer inspection, a snapshot of the painting. "*Ma questo e una fotografia!*" I protest.

"'*La Nativita con i Santi Francesco e Lorenzo,*' *si!*" the old man insists, firmly clasping the 1,000 Lire note, lest I try and retrieve it.

Perhaps it's my faulty Italian. "*Non capisco!* I don't understand! *Dove è l'originale?*"

"*Ah si!*" he nods, finally fathoming the source of my confusion. "*E stato rubato!* Stolen!" he shrugs matter-of-factly, as if relating an unfortunate fact of life.

It's a bad joke. Unable to believe my eyes, I don't know whether to laugh or to cry. I've travelled the length of Italy's boot to see a painting that isn't there, a phantom masterpiece which this old man has watched over much of his adult life; yet to him, nothing's missing. Three centuries ago, a man of talent mixed his pigments on a pallet and applied them to cloth, capturing the image of a couple of local vagrants disguised as saints, an urchin masquerading as an angel, and a cow looking on as a *signorina* makes ready to suckle a reclining infant. Seeing is believing. The image draped with the halo of sanctity engraved itself on the sacristan's consciousness. The painting's subsequent disappearance is beside the point, the canvas itself a disposable negative in the photo-optic chemistry of faith.

Not that I am quite capable of reasoning things out at the time, but I understand in some wordless way that I've been on the wrong track, hunting down illusions instead of going after the real thing.

More than a quarter century has gone by, the snapshot having long since fallen off the wall of the church, the old sacristan having carried his image of The Nativity to the grave, and yours truly, the disappointed pilgrim, having grown up and forgotten the fever of his teens — when suddenly, out of nowhere leaps an Italian Rumpelstiltskin, Marino Mannoia, a messenger from the past whose name evokes an unsavory onomatopoeic mix of mania and ennui.

How often do we encounter one of the many invisible agents of that hodge-podge of chance and choice called destiny, an individual who, unbeknownst to him, and by an act of no immediate concern to us alters the ground rules of the game?

And now with a final brush stroke worthy of the master, this unlikely angel straight out of Caravaggio's dubious circle of friends completes a tableau I've never seen but which has moved me profoundly, thus resolving the mystery of the missing canvas — a mystery obliquely linking the late sacristan of the Church of San Lorenzo, a painter, a thief, a 17-year-old aesthete and a convalescent middle-aged pilgrim in tea-stained pajamas, rekindling the latter's faith in miracles.

Nostalgia for the Norm:
Observations in the Vale and Vector of the Virus
(An Afterword)

It's late yet again. And again, I survey the silence, inverting wakefulness and sleep. Again, in place of dreaming, I listen to the refrigerator humming. The construction site that had been growing like a giant metal bean stalk outside my window, down the block, has suspended activity, its girders rearing midair untrussed. Who knows when work will begin again? The street has fallen silent, all the foul language formerly howled has been sucked back into the absent throats of nonexistent passersby. Unaccustomed to silence — to think that I would ever miss the very things that bothered me most!

New Yorkers like to tout our town as the center of the universe. We would gladly have passed on the privilege of being the epicenter of the outbreak this time around.

I live in the rarefied environs of Greenwich Village. On the surface not much has changed. The birds are singing. The flowers have burst their buds. It's spring again. Time to shed winter doldrums. But such transient seasonal distress has since been replaced by a seasonless dread.

In the beginning of the pandemic, masked- and gloved-up, I regularly ventured out. Most stores have since shut down for the duration; though deemed essential enterprises, along with the pharmacies, bodegas, and supermarkets, the head shops are open for business — go figure! All restaurants, bars and other non-essential businesses are gated or boarded up, with printed or handwritten signs, some affecting a friendly personal tone, most perfunctory, announcing temporary closure. But how temporary is temporary? How many will ever reopen?

At the start of it all, I witnessed a white-bearded man with a turban in Biblical attire blasting on a ram's horn, a self-appointed prophet, I suppose, proclaiming the 11th plague. (He has more recently been replaced by a bagpiper sounding a daily dirge for the departed.) For a lark, early on, two young men donned rabbit masks and hopped about, photographed by a third. "Don't forget to hold up the sign!" the photographer cried. Whereupon the two dutifully flashed placards with hashtags "#Come to the Doom's Day Dinner." This is The Village, after all, and you expect such benign eccentricities.

But dinners, like all other gatherings, have since become taboo. The few souls I pass nowadays on short nocturnal jaunts are either dog-walkers, or aimless beggars with no place to go. After doling out dollars each time you step out, you get good at reading a shadow from afar — if it shuffles, limps or stalls, keep your distance. The faceless phantoms, like myself, walk at a steady, rapid clip. We keep as far as possible apart, and exchange fleeting looks, each viewing the other as a virtual threat, a potential carrier of infection.

The other day, for no apparent reason, an angry teenager walked up to me and butted me in the chest. It was not a friendly greeting.

Is this the new norm?

I have stomped the same circuit of streets and exhausted novelty on my limited nightly trajectories. Upon returning home I escape into my imaginings. Of late I have tried to envision our microscopic adversary, variously depicted on internet sites either as an abstract expressionist pattern of tinted stains, or in 3-D representations as cauliflower-like globs, or else as spherical entities with extended knobs, minuscule invaders, streamlined and downsized since the advent of H.G. Wells' *War of the Worlds*, but invaders all the same.

Despite all, I cannot help but be awestruck by the dogged determination of the virus, its resilience and stubborn resolve to proliferate.

Its appellation derives from a Latin word meaning 'slimy liquid' or 'poison.' When not squatting in and freeloading on an infected cell, viruses apparently loll about as discrete particles, or virions, vagrant molecules of DNA or RNA with nothing to do but dangle.

Microbiologists the world over are busy studying the genetic code, decoding the viral dialect. Whoever deciphers it first and manages to establish its secret fallibility will surely win a Nobel Prize.

I once interviewed the late Nobel laureate Baruch Blumberg, a geneticist who shared the 1976 Nobel Prize in Physiology or Medicine for his pioneering role in the discovery of the hepatitis B virus and the development of a vaccine to combat it. In the course of our interview, he decried the bellicose notion of "battling disease." "It's not a helpful metaphor," he cautioned.

I imagine hordes of microscopic marauders circling the city, storming the gates of unguarded mouths, eyes and noses. The threat looms largest at night, when darkness closes in and I mull over the latest tally of casualties, hoping not to become a statistic myself.

Like everyone else, I too long for the vaccine as a valiant knight to rescue us from the scourge. But like it or not, viruses are here to stay. They will keep mutating, as all life forms do, reemerging in new, ever more virulent iterations. They are our unseen neighbors. We share the same strands of life.

The human body hosts "good" bacteria that aid in digestion and other physiological functions. So, too, apparently, do we host so-called bacteriophages, viruses lodged in the mucus membrane lining in the digestive, respiratory and reproductive tracts that destroy invasive bacteria. Phages have been utilized to treat dysentery, sepsis, salmonella infections and skin infections, among other maladies.

What if, I wonder, we could someday genetically reengineer malignant viruses to render them good neighbors, helpful partners cohabiting the same organism they otherwise ravage? It's a hopeful science fiction fantasy, no doubt, but there are worse ways to wrestle with the dread.

Outside, meanwhile, the early birds are twittering up a storm. An entrenched city slicker, I long for the sounds I once loathed, the car horns and curses hurled at all hours, the thump of construction, the clink and clang of business as usual.

Post Script

This book was compiled in lockdown as a virtual SOS in a bottle in the Time of the Virus. May it be retrieved by receptive readers in the future, when social distancing will, hopefully, be a morbid memento mori, streets open for strolling, friends once again embraced, and masks worn only, of necessity, by surgeons in the ER, superheroes on screen, celebrants at costume balls, and hoodlums on a heist.

New York, January 15, 2021

Acknowledgments

"The Spirit Tree," "The Third Line," "A Forgotten Game," The Sultry Scent of Formaldehyde," "Wurst Lust," "Nostalgia for the Norm: Observations in the Vale and Vector of the Virus" and "Never Mind the Notes, Just Worry 'bout the Chords 'n Intervals" all originally appeared on the website Mr. Beller's Neighborhood. "Nostalgia for the Norm: Observations in the Vale and Vector of the Virus" was republished on the website Love in the Time of Coronavirus. "Rough Cuts" first ran in *The Brooklyn Rail* and was included in my book *Footprints in Wet Cement*, as were parts of "New York's Unreal Estate." "How the French Test Their Mettle" was first published in the journal *France Guide*. "The Importance of Getting Goofy" first ran in *The Christian Science Monitor*. "Adventures in the French Digestive Tract," "New York' Unreal Estate" and "The Catalan Lottery Ticket" all were first issued on the website *Panorama, The Journal of Intelligent Travel*. "Splendor on the Plate: A Taste of Rural Piemonte" was originally published in the journal *Hidden Europe*. "In the Golden Valley of Ale" first appeared in *The Boston Globe*. "Still Brewing Strong: Café Culture in Vienna" appeared in various iterations in *The Washington Post*, *The New Mexican*, *The Columbus Dispatch*, *The San Jose Mercury News*, and *Vienna Magazine*. "Robbing the Seagulls of their Virgin Shriek" was first featured in *The Buffalo News*. "Till Death Do Us Part in the Delta: A Mississippi Odyssey" was originally published on the website *Shaking Like a Mountain*. "Confessions of a Born-Again Cowboy in France" debuted on the website *Worldhum.com* (A division of The Travel Channel) and was subsequently reissued in *The Best Travel Writing 2009*. "Balzac's Telling Scratches" appeared under a different title on the website *Literary Hub*. "Measurements of the Iron Lady" was originally published under a different title in the journal *Rendezvous en France*. "Vanishing Vienna" first ran in the journal *Grand Tour* and was selected for inclusion in *The Best Travel Writing, Volume 9*. "From Vienna with Love (And Other Mixed Emotions"" was published in *The Paris Review*. "Berchtesgaden: Who Let the Dogs Out?" first ran, under a different title, in the webzine *Citizen Culture Magazine*. "Holy Land Blues" first appeared in the book *Encounters with the Middle East*, and was subsequently included in *The Best Travel Writing 2008*. "Senegal: Impressions" first ran in the journal *New Observations*. "Snapshots and Souvenirs" was first published in the British-based journal *European Judaism*. The title text "Epiphany of a Middle-Aged Pilgrim in Tea-Stained Pajamas" was first published in *The Brooklyn Rail* and subsequently reissued in *The Best Travel Writing 2010*.

Warm thanks, as always, to my publisher, Mark Givens, my brother, Harold Wortsman, a reader whose judgment I trust and who designed the splendid cover, and Ricky Owens, who makes me look younger in the author's photo.

About the Author

Dubbed "a 20th-century Brother Grimm" (Bloomsbury Review) and "a delinquent Hans Christian Andersen" (by playwright Mark O'Donnell), Peter Wortsman is the author of work in multiple modes, including three books of short fiction, *A Modern Way To Die* (1991, second edition, 2020), *Footprints in Wet Cement* (2017), and *Stimme und Atem / Out of Breath, Out of Mind* (2019); a travel memoir, *Ghost Dance in Berlin, A Rhapsody in Gray* (2013); a novel, *Cold Earth Wanderers* (2014); and a work of nonfiction, *The Caring Heirs of Doctor Samuel Bard* (2019). He collaborated with artist Harold Wortsman on an artists' book, *it-t=i* (2004).

He is also the author of two stage plays, *The Tattooed Man Tells All* (2000), produced by the Silverthorne Theater Company, 2018, filmed, 2020, and produced in German translation by the Deutsches Theater in Göttingen, 2021, and *Burning Words*, produced in 2006 by the Hampshire Shakespeare Company, at the Northampton Center for the Arts, in Northampton, Mass., and again in 2014, in German translation, at the Kulturhaus Osterfeld, in Pforzheim, Germany.

His travel writing has run in such major newspapers as *The New York Times* and the *Los Angeles Times*, and was included five years in a row in *The Best Travel Writing*, 2008-2012, and again in 2016.

He is also a critically acclaimed translator of literary works from German into English, including *Posthumous Papers of a Living Author*, by Robert Musil, now in its third edition (1988, 2005, 2009); *Telegrams of the Soul: Selected Prose of Peter Altenberg* (2005); *Travel Pictures, by Heinrich Heine* (2008); *Selected*

Prose of Heinrich von Kleist (2010); *Selected Tales of the Brothers Grimm* (2013); *Tales of the German Imagination, From the Brothers Grimm to Ingeborg Bachmann* (2013), an anthology which he also edited and annotated; and *Konundrum, Selected Prose of Franz Kafka* (2016).

He was the recipient of the 1985 Beard's Fund Short Story Award, the 2008 Geertje Potash-Suhr SCALG-Prosapreis (a prize for short original fiction in German) awarded by the Society for Contemporary American Literature in German, the 2012 Gold Grand Prize for Best Travel Story of the Year in the Solas Awards Competition, and a 2014 Independent Publishers Book Award (IPPY). A former fellow of the Fulbright Foundation (1973), the Thomas J. Watson Foundation (1974), he was a Holtzbrinck Fellow at the American Academy in Berlin (2010), and a fellow of the Österreichische Gesesellschaft für Literatur (2016).

AUTHOR PHOTO BY RICKY OWENS

Other Books By Peter Wortsman

A Modern Way to Die, smallstories and microtales, Fromm Publishing International, 1991; second edition, Pelekinesis, 2020

it - t = i, an artists' book, produced in collaboration with graphic artist, Harold Wortsman, here and now press, 2004

Ghost Dance in Berlin, A Rhapsody in Gray, a travel memoir, Travelers' Tales, 2013; *Geistertanz in Berlin,* a German translation by Werner Rauch, Palm Art Press, 2021

Tales of the German Imagination, from The Brothers Grimm to Ingeborg Bachmann, an anthology, Penguin Classics, 2013; *Tales of the German Imagination from the Brothers Grimm to Ingeborg Bachmann,* by Peter Wortsman - translator and editor, an audiobook, narrated by Jonathan Keeble, Penguin Classics, 2021

Cold Earth Wanderers, a novel, Pelekinesis, 2014

Brennende Worte, the German translation of *Burning Words,* a play by Peter Wortsman, translated from the English by Peter Torberg, Kulturhaus Osterfeld, Pforzheim, Germany, 2014

New York, NY, 1978, a photo essay, produced in collaboration with photographer Jean-Luc Dubin, Les Editions Dumerchez, 2016

Footprints in Wet Cement, a collection of short prose, Pelekinesis, 2017

The Caring Heirs of Dr. Samuel Bard (Selected Profiles of Distinguished Graduates of the Columbia University Vagelos College of Physicians and Surgeons), Columbia University Press, 2019

Stimme und Atem/ Out of Breath...Out of Mind, a bilingual German-English collection of stories originally composed in German, PalmArt Press, Berlin, 2019

Selected Translations:

Posthumous Papers of a Living Author, by Robert Musil, Volume One of Eridanos Library, 1988; second edition, Penguin 20th Century Classics, 1995; third edition, Archipelago Books, 2006; *Flypaper*, an excerpt, Penguin Mini-Classics, 2011

Peter Schlemiel, The Man Who Sold His Shadow, by Adelbert von Chamisso, Fromm International Publishing Co., 1993

Telegrams of the Soul, Selected Prose of Peter Altenberg, Archipelago Books, NY, 2005

Selected Short Prose of Heinrich von Kleist, Archipelago Books, 2010

Selected Tales of the Brothers Grimm, Archipelago Books, 2013

Konundrum, Selected Prose of Franz Kafka, Archipelago Books, 2016

Intimate Ties, by Robert Musil, a new translation, Archipelago Books, Brooklyn, NY, 2019

Hinkemann, a tragedy by Ernst Toller, a new translation, Berlinica Books, 2019

The Golden Pot and Other Selected Tales, by E.T.A. Hoffmann, Archipelago Books, forthcoming 2022

Praise For Peter Wortsman

"The behavior of the people [in 'Snapshots and Souvenirs'] was wonderfully human and moving—the sort of thing even the best writers find it almost impossible to invent. The unexpected in human behavior is difficult to take out of the air, as opposed to the usual, which anyone can invent. So that it is precisely these unforeseen details which establish the authenticity of the text, and which give it its literary value... excellent."

–Paul Bowles, author of *The Sheltering Sky*

"*A Modern Way to Die* is a fantastic book and I thoroughly enjoyed it. I have never read anything quite like this, but my enjoyment was due to more than just novelty, it was a response to marvelous writing, wonderful craft, and the breath of imagination... [Wortsman] succeeded so well in his craft and art that it reads 'artless' and 'spontaneous,' which to me is the highest of compliments."

–Hubert Selby, Jr., author of *Last Exit to Brooklyn*

"Wortsman achieves a level of spontaneity and accessibility...to which most writers can only aspire."

–David Ulin, *The L.A. Weekly*

"Wortsman hangs with the masters."

–A. Scott Cardwell, *The Boston Phoenix*

"His work reminded me some of E.B. White's *New Yorker* stuff—observations turned into little reads but with a modernist twist."

–Ruth Lopez, *The New Mexican*

"Peter Wortsman, in the light of day, seems able to connect the power of the dream narrative to conscious language to create unique works that walk a curious line between fiction and poetry."

–Russell Edson, author of *The Tunnel: Selected Poems of Russell Edson*

"A darkly comic folktale for a dysfunctional future, or a nightmare fable for disobedient children, Peter Wortsman's *Cold Earth Wanderers* sends a disaffected teenager down the elevator shaft of an up-and-down human habitat cut off from its roots, on an unsettling journey to recover what was lost. Against the myth of mindless upward progress Wortsman pits the subversive grotesquerie of open-ended lateral exploration."

–Geoffrey O'Brien, author of *The Phantom Empire* and *Stolen Glimpses, Captive Shadows*

112 Harvard Ave #65

Claremont, CA 91711 USA

pelekinesis@gmail.com

www.pelekinesis.com

Pelekinesis titles are available through Small
Press Distribution, Baker & Taylor, Ingram, Bertrams,
and directly from the publisher's website.

CPSIA information can be obtained
at www.ICGtesting.com
Printed in the USA
FSHW011113301121
86556FS

9 781949 790474